TRUE CRIME STORIES

Hannah J. Tidy

Murders, Disappearances, and Serial Killers
Twisted Tales of True Crime

TABLE OF CONTENTS

INTRODUCTION

"Killers are your sons, we are your husbands, we are everywhere. And there will be more of your children dead tomorrow."

— Ted Bundy

While infamous serial killer Ted Bundy may not be the symbol of virtue that we would expect to see quoted in the introduction to a book, he is undoubtedly an expert in what it takes to be a cold-blooded killer. His words possibly also hold a clue as to why we are obsessed with people like him and the victims they rip away from the world in the most brutal of ways. True crime is no longer merely a genre applicable in the publishing world or a sign in the library that indicates the shelf on which books covering such topics are kept. True crime has become a world of its own. It has created a community of like-minded armchair detectives, and the outcome of that has been the creation of television shows, podcasts, YouTube channels, and online forums that feed our insatiable desire to know more. Some may find the conversion of criminal cases into forms of entertainment obscene, but the truth is that true crime when done well, can give a victim a voice that they didn't have in life.

Giving the victims a voice is the honorable core of what true-crime content is capable of achieving in the world. The entertainment element is undeniably there, but the psychology behind why we love true crime goes so much deeper than that. Humanity focuses on the fight between good and evil, and we have documented this battle since the first known written record. For an ancient man, the struggle may have represented a fight between angels and demons, and today, our epitome of evil is a person who is capable of committing what we perceive to be the ultimate crime — the taking of a life. Evil fascinates us for many reasons. We want to understand where it comes from and how it forms. We want to know how an innocent baby, born into this world as innocent as any other, grows into a deviant. Perhaps most importantly, we want to know how to avoid it. We may even think that by understanding evil, we can guarantee that it will never touch our lives. The news media have only intensified our interest in the personal tragedies of strangers. Today, we are bombarded 24/7, predominantly by stories of crime, and this only serves to accentuate our interest.

Some experts believe that crime is an inevitable part of our society, and as such, we have no choice but to understand the people who commit these crimes. It is as integral to societal composition as understanding religion or sexuality. This opinion is a rather interesting perspective, as it may allow us to consider our true-crime obsession as a positive contribution to society. Human beings are, after all, designed to pay attention to things that could harm us. This instinct is how we learned which plants not to eat and that snakes are not always harmless.

This evolutionary perspective may play a role in our interest in true crime. If we, as a society, pay attention to what poses a threat to us, then we will be more likely to recognize it in the future.

So, why do women seem more interested in true crime than men? Well, the answer to that question may lay in our innate need to protect ourselves. Although men are more likely to fall victim to homicide, women are more likely to be killed by intimate partners. Some of the most horrific crimes involve female victims. This reality is no secret to the fairer sex, of course, and it is this knowledge, it seems, that may drive female audiences to consume true-crime content at a higher rate than their male counterparts. It is thought that women seek a sense of preparedness by listening to the stories of those that have fallen foul of evil people. Although this may not be a conscious action, women feel safer knowing how others fell victim, and this helps them to believe that they can avoid falling into the same trap.

I believe it's not just murders that interest us. Unsolved disappearances and other mysteries in the true-crime realm are just as tantalizing, and this boils down to our human need for closure. We like to be able to solve problems, and a mystery without resolution is just the type of problem we would like to put in a box and top with a bow and a label that reads, "Solved." Human beings want things to make sense, and that is what draws us to unsolved mysteries — the opportunity to set things right and restore balance to the world. It is perhaps also this need for continuity that spurs our interest in true crime.

Author and victim's advocate Billy Jensen refers to it as "wanting to know that the monster is in a cage." In our minds, justice for victims equates to justice for all. If we can see that the monster didn't get away with their evil acts, perhaps we can believe, if even just for a moment, that evil will not find us too.

My name is Hannah J Tidy. I am a true crime and paranormal genre author. After experiencing a traumatic unsolved disappearance of a loved one, I was motivated to write about true crime stories of others, even looking to the paranormal for answers. Through my writing, I hope to bring awareness to such cases and help to give the victims a voice, the stories covered in this book span the spectrum of mystery from serial killers to murders and disappearances. I seek to present lesser-known true crime facts and delve deeper into the more well-known cases.

I believe it is always essential when presenting true crime content, to have a balance between information on the perpetrator and information on the victim. While we are acting as a voice for the victim, it is equally important to understand who the perpetrator was and how they grew up. This approach is, in no way, done to excuse behavior. We talk about a perpetrator's past to understand their actions better. Focusing too much on the childhood of a perpetrator also has its pitfalls, though. It is the old nature versus nurture debate. Are killers made, or are they born? In most of the cases in which we have a background on perpetrators, you will likely see that the answer is a combination of the two. No matter what mental illnesses you are born susceptible to, treatment and choice are always available. It is when that dangerous birthright, in combination with an environment that promotes abuse and additional trauma, that the toxic combination of deadly nature and deadly nurture, begins to emerge.

As we delve into the cases we have selected, our focus is always on the victim. While it is crucial to provide the details of the case, specific details do not need to be too far expanded on, and if it is not in the interests of the victim, then it is best not to do so. One of the main pitfalls of the true-crime community is sensationalism, and this should be something that independent true crime content creators avoid at all costs. Sensationalism and headline-grabbing statements are the domain of mainstream media. While they, too, have a role to play in reporting crime and giving the victims a voice, this should never be the directive of non-mainstream media. As creators and as the audience, we have a responsibility to the victim to ensure that we tell their story as respectfully and truthfully as possible. This responsibility is the basis of how I have structured these stories, and I trust that you will enjoy the content I have created for you.

CHAPTER 1

HOUSE OF HORRORS

A small voice crackles through the line as the 911 operator answers. Jordan Turpin is 17 years old, but the hesitance and fear in her voice disguise her age. When authorities saw her for the first time, they believed she was no older than 10. As though Jordan is trying to get everything out as quickly as possible. As soon as the operator asks her what the problem is, she launches into a report from hell.

Jordan told the 911 operator the most unbelievably cruel conditions in which they lived. Jordan and her 12 siblings held against their will, some chained, and all are starved and severely abused. Their captors are not strangers or psychotic kidnappers. The perpetrators are their parents. Within minutes Perris County police officers descend on the house for a welfare check. What they find will be beyond belief and will horrify the world.

Strange Beginnings

Louise Turpin met her husband-to-be in the 1980s when she was a very young teenager. David Turpin was already in his 20s, but the age gap meant nothing to either of them and as soon as Louise turned 16, they married. For Louise, it was a way to escape a severely abusive childhood in which, as her sister would later claim, they were subjected to sexual abuse by their grandfather with their mother's knowledge and consent. In David, Louise likely saw the promise of a stable future. He was smart and successful and earned a good salary as an engineer.

In the beginning, Louise's family was welcomed into the Turpin's home to visit. David would fly in her siblings regularly. However, this contact soon started to wane. Within the first 15 years of their marriage, they had eight children. Louise's visiting siblings would say that although they did not witness anything that they would term abuse in those early years, the Turpins were extremely strict with their children.

The outside world saw a picture of wealth and success. To everyone else, it appeared that the family was happy and well-rounded. Louise's in-person contact with her siblings became sporadic, and the family became more isolated. The only window into their lives was the social media posts that Louise would make. Pictures of trips to Disneyland and several vacations to Las Vegas to renew their wedding vows showed smiling children, all meticulously dressed in identical clothes.

By 1998, the Turpin family completely cut themselves off from friends and family. The couple would also declare bankruptcy at this time, despite David's above-average salary. Later investigations would indicate that their financial problems were not so much a shortage of money but rather highly irresponsible and lavish spending by the pair. The children saw none of this lavishness, though.

Initially, some of the Turpin children did attend school, but by 1998, the couple decided that they would home-school the children instead. The family lived in a rural area of Texas for a decade, and their neighbors would later report feeling that something was off about the family. A family who lived closest to the Turpin house allowed their daughter to play with the children on the rare occasion that they appeared in the front yard. The children were filthy, the neighbor said. So dirty that the neighbor thought one child was wearing white gloves, until realizing it was a result of the child's hands only washed up to her wrists, and the rest of her body caked with filth. In her 911 call many years later, Jordan Turpin would admit that her parents had only allowed her and her siblings to bathe once a year.

(*60 Minutes Australia, 2019*).

Piles of Dirty Diapers

By the time the Turpin couple left the house in Texas, they had added another four children to the family. The alleged impetus for that move was the escape of one of their children. One of the female children had escaped the house and tried to get help when they still lived in Texas.

Sadly, the people she approached for help thought that she was mentally challenged and did not believe her story. They returned her to her parents. In reality, the girl was so malnourished that she was unable to speak correctly. The isolation from the outside world also made the children painfully shy. There was no homeschooling given to the children, as the Turpins claimed. Instead, decades later, when rescuing the children, they were found barely able to read and write.

When the Turpin family vacated their Texas home, they left it behind in a horrific state. The house looked as though it had not been cleaned in years, piles of dirty diapers scattered throughout the living areas. The walls caked in filth, patches of human excrement found on carpets. Deceased pets found decomposing within the house. They also allegedly found chains attached to the beds as well. Sadly, the condition of this house only came to light after rescuing the children.

Having left Texas, Louise, David, and their 12 children moved to California. This move signaled a change in the Turpin couple. Their abuse escalated, and their ordinarily strict religious lifestyle suddenly decayed. They started to drink heavily and brought other couples into the home for partner-swapping sexual encounters. In 2016, Louise gave birth to their 13th child, and there are reports that she had ambitions of starring in a reality television series with her family.

(*Killelea, 2020*).

Horrific Abuse

In January 2018, 17-year-old Jordan Turpin and one of her sisters found a deactivated cell phone and escaped the house. Jordan's sibling became terrified of the consequences if they were caught and returned to the house. Jordan continued and made the call that would eventually save her siblings' lives.

(*Inside Edition, 2019*).

While the true extent of the abuse the children suffered will, likely, only come out in trickles as the children begin to heal and work through their trauma. The pieces we do know are horrifying enough besides forced to live in filthy conditions and denying them schooling. The children were also regularly chained to their beds for hours on end. Stains on their mattresses indicated that they had not been allowed toilet breaks either. The children were beaten and starved. Food deprivation is terrible enough, but their parents took it a sadistic step further.

They would eat in front of their starving children or place food on the kitchen counters for them to see—but not eat. If any of them ate food without permission, they punished them severely. The only activity that the children were allowed to participate in was journaling, and the police found large piles of notebooks when they searched the house. Brand new toys left in their packaging as a way to taunt the children. If they dared touch the toys, there would be hell to pay.

All of the children were severely malnourished and mentally underdeveloped. The oldest Turpin child was 29 years old at the time of the rescue, but weighed only 80 pounds and had the mentality of a first-grader. Medical investigations would prove that she had been born completely healthy from a physical and mental perspective. Her condition was a direct result of nearly 30 years of abuse and deprivation. There also seemed to be a distinct difference in how the parents treated the female children compared to the males. Although the male children were starved and subjected to abuse, the older ones were allowed small freedoms. One older Turpin male was even allowed to attend community college. That said, his mother would drive him to his classes, wait outside for him until school was over, and then bring him straight home.

Justice

After their rescue, the state took care of the Turpin children, managing their recovery very carefully to ensure they learned to trust the people caring for them. The court charged David and Louise Turpin with 14 different felony counts of false imprisonment and torture. Although they initially protested their innocence, in 2019, the couple admitted their guilt, and they were each sentenced to 25 years to life in prison. They will have the possibility of parole after serving 22 years of their sentence.

The Turpin children continue to make a slow and steady recovery. Although they will likely never achieve their potential (*should they have had a better start in life*), they are certainly making the best of their second chance.

One of the most tragic parts of this case is all of the missed opportunities for an earlier rescue. There were red flags everywhere, that could have helped the children sooner. While it's easy to look back in hindsight, Texas's state surely should have made *someone* consider whether that was a suitable environment for children and speak up.

The first escape made by one of the children in Texas was another dashed chance when neighbors merely accepted Louise and David's deceitful explanation for their daughter's behavior. Countless neighbors came forward after the rescue to say that they had noticed odd things about the family, yet no one called authorities. The explanation for this seems to be that people don't want to accuse someone falsely, and they don't want to stick their nose too far into other people's business and lives. The truth is, though, that when children are involved, we have a responsibility to act. All it takes is one phone call to a local police station.

The Turpin children will all have very different healing journeys ahead of them. It is probable that, despite the horrors they experienced, some will find it difficult to separate themselves from their parents and may maintain voluntary contact. This behavior is not uncommon in abuse cases as victims struggle to rationalize the feelings of attachment they develop toward their abusers.

Many have questioned why it took so long for one of the children to come forward. So many of the children were over eighteen—technically adults—that the public found it difficult to understand why they had stayed inside the house. Besides the physical restraints put on them, the mental constraints were likely far more powerful. It is the abusers' nature to isolate their victims and ensure they have no means of escape. The children probably had no idea who police officers were or could trust the outside world for help.

The resounding question, in this case, remains: Why would parents do this to their children? While both David and Louise were mentally fit to stand trial, this does not discount the possibility that mental health issues were at play. The existence of such mental health issues also does not excuse their actions. David does seem to have been the dominant person in the relationship, and he was the only one who worked outside the home. He also held all of the financial control. So, there is a possibility that Louise felt like she had no other choice but to comply. Many of the children disagree with this. Stating that their mother regularly abused them without their father being present. She was often the instigator for new and horrendous forms of torture.

While we may never really know why the Turpins did what they did to their children, it is evident that the ridiculous duration of the abuse was utterly unnecessary. Missed opportunities by authorities and individuals exasperated the situation. In the end, though, the responsibility lies with David and Louise, who chose to bring children into this world and then chose to torture and abuse them systematically. They are now where they belong, and we can only hope that their children will live happy and healthy lives.

CHAPTER 2

VANISHING CHILDREN

I t is close to midnight on the 13th of September 1990 in the tiny town of Bowraville. The street, which houses an Aboriginal community nicknamed The Mission, is quiet, except for one house. The house party has been buzzing for a few hours already, attended by most of the street's residents. The neighbors drink alcohol, laugh, and revel in the clear, crisp Australian spring night.

They have few worries at this moment — the stressors of living in difficult economic times and the poor treatment they often receive from authorities, forgotten at the bottom of a bottle of beer. Within moments though, events will start to unfold, which will rip this community apart. This moment of celebration would be the last for a long time, and even when they begin to pick up the pieces, things will never entirely be the same in Bowraville.

A 16-year-old girl, Colleen Walker-Craig, is among the partygoers. She's not a resident of Bowraville, though. She's visiting family there from Sawtell, a coastal town just 44 miles from Bowraville. Colleen is pretty. Her brown curls stick to her face. Although the temperature is not unusually warm, the crowd creates humidity, which she feels the need to escape and cool off. A group of partygoers would later report seeing Colleen walking into the night, away from the house. No one called after her. There was no need. Bowraville was safe. The residents of The Mission were like family, and so, they let her go. They had no idea that they would never see her alive again.

Where Is Colleen?

The next day, when Colleen's family realized that the young girl had never returned to her family's home after the party, they immediately went to the police. The police insisted that Colleen, *being a teenager*, must have gone off on her own and would likely return soon. Despite her family's protestations of this being totally unlike the quiet, responsible teenager, the police refused to open a missing person's case. Performing no official searches for her, and taking no formal police action in those crucial early days after Colleen's disappearance

(*Scheikowski, 2018*).

Relations between authorities, including police and the Aboriginal communities, were always strained. The native Australian citizens feel stigmatized as a society of criminals and targeted whenever a crime takes place. When an Aboriginal person falls victim to a crime, they believe the police are less likely to react. Many Aboriginal societies in Australia suffer in poverty-stricken communities. Drugs and alcohol become prevalent problems in any area where the reality of life is too difficult to bear without something to take the edge off. It is this lifestyle, police say, causes many Aboriginal people to become high-risk victims. Authorities claim they will judge any missing person's case by the risk-level of the disappeared person.

For this reason, the police say they do not always jump into action when any teenager goes missing. Teenagers run away all the time. Aboriginal teenagers, they claim, do so even more frequently. The community feels this explanation is ridiculous. Many countries worldwide experience this inequity in policing when it comes to native or lower economic communities. It's a phenomenon we could term invisible *victims*, and it's not just the police that behaves differently when these communities suffer crime incidents. The media is less likely to publish the story of a missing Aboriginal girl than a girl of the same age having gone missing from an upper-class suburb. The public, at large, has seemingly been equally brainwashed into believing that there are victims more worthy of justice than others. It is a phenomenon that would have devastating consequences for the Bowraville community.

Colleen Walker-Craig never to be seen again. Her family did what they could to search for her, but with limited resources, *in the end*, they could only cling to the hope that the teenager perhaps ran off and started a new life somewhere. There hope would shatter when less than a month later, it happened again.

Cries in the Night

Four-year-old Evelyn Greenup slept peacefully on the night of the 4th of October, 1990, curled up in her bed at her grandmother's house. Still, there was a party going on outside her bedroom door, so Evelyn would occasionally wake and lay staring into the darkness listening to the adults laughing and talking loudly. Evelyn was the cousin of Colleen Walker-Craig, who disappeared on a night not dissimilar to this one less than a month earlier. Evelyn's grandmother would later say, she may have heard her granddaughter cry out that evening, but she wasn't sure. What was certain, though, was that by the time the adults started to roll out of bed the next morning, their heads pounding from the previous night's entertainment, little Evelyn was gone. At some time during the night, Evelyn was either taken or left the house of her own. As with her cousin's case, police were slow to act and hesitant to file a missing person's report, claiming another family member could have taken Evelyn. Eventually, under pressure from the community, four-year-old Evelyn's case was considered slightly more seriously, and the case opened.

Months after both disappearances, the family would lose any hope they had of 16-year-old Colleen's safe return. Fears intensified around Evelyn's whereabouts when a hiker found something near the Nambucca River. It was the clothing that Colleen Walker-Craig was wearing on the night of her disappearance, weighed down by rocks, inside the river. The family had to accept that Colleen did not wander off to start a new life somewhere else, and although her body was never recovered, it seemed clear there was some foul play involved. Little Evelyn's cherubic face still shone out from *missing posters* across Bowraville, but it would not be long until a third disappearance set the course of possible answers.

The Caravan

The Bowraville community attempted to continue with their lives despite the deepening mystery around the two missing local girls. The year 1990 ticked over into a new year, and the residents of what was becoming a seemingly doomed street hoped that 1991 would bring some resolution and closure. Sadly, before it could, it would bring more pain.

Sixteen-year-old Clinton Speedy-Duroux was a strapping young man who looked after his appearance. He was known for always wearing his favorite sneakers. Clinton had been staying with his girlfriend in a yellow Viscount Caravan. On the evening of 31st of January 1991, Clinton attended a house party on the same road Evelyn and Colleen disappeared. He also was never seen again. Clinton became the third Bowraville child to vanish into the night, but his disappearance would spark revelations that would tear the community apart.

Local police had no choice but to start paying attention to what was happening in the Bowraville community. They could perhaps ignore the disappearance of one child, but with Colleen's clothing now having been found and another two children have gone without a trace, it seemed clear there was something very dark happening at *The Mission*.

Just 18 days after his disappearance, police discovered the remains of Clinton Speedy-Duroux. Although severely decomposed, his remains were identifiable. Police located Clinton in bushland near Congarinni Road, seven kilometers from the Bowraville house from where he disappeared. Clinton's body was clothed only in a pair of shorts, and inside those shorts, police found a piece of fabric. The investigating officer recognized the cloth as matching a pillowcase that traced back to the caravan Clinton shared with his girlfriend during the days before his disappearance. The police now knew that whoever killed Clinton had access to that caravan. The trailer stood on the property of a local white family, and the primary resident was 24-year-old laborer Jay Hart. Jay's identity, protected for many years, due to the legal wranglings that would play out in the years to come. In transcripts and even in media articles referred to him as Mr. XX. Yet, in 2016, a podcast series by a journalist from the media outlet *The Australian* would dive deeply into the case and reveal Mr. XX's true identity.

(Wahlquist, 2016).

Who Is Jay Hart?

The investigating officer on the case described the caravan Jay Hart lived in as meager. There were the bare necessities for living, including the linen he had recognized but little else. Unfortunately, due to the police's slow response, Jay Hart continued to live in this caravan for two weeks after Clinton's disappearance. By the time police made the connection, by finding Clintons remains. Hart moved out of the trailer, taking much of the contents with him. We may never know how much evidence was lost due to the passage of time and the police's failure to contain the caravan.

Jay described as an ordinarily quiet young man, but in the podcast, his former girlfriend, *Alison*, describes him becoming extremely violent when he drank. The woman claims she was assaulted on several occasions by Jay, but because she was of Aboriginal ethnicity and Jay was not, she never pressed charges. Alison claims she saw no point as she didn't feel she would have the police's support. When Clinton disappeared, Jay was working in an animal hide factory moving carcasses after workers skinned them. Although racial segregation was still a real phenomenon in South West Australia at this time, Jay mixed easily with all the residents of Bowraville and was a regular at local parties in The Mission. He would bring alcohol and allegedly marijuana, and despite his imposingly significant presence, this, neighbors said, made him a welcome guest.

Jay was known to have been in several relationships with girls from The Mission, and he was known to be a highly sexualized man. This fact would become significant in later legal battles.

Jay's connection to the caravan and his further connection to Clinton soon prompted the police to arrest him and charge him with the boy's murder. The autopsy on Clinton's body showed someone impaled him with a sharp object. The object went straight through his skull and into his brain, killing him instantly. This manner of death is not dissimilar to how they slaughter animals in *animal hide* factories in which Jay worked. Police were not blind to the fact that Jay Hart had connections to the two other missing children as well.

Colleen's sister would come forward to identify Jay Hart as a man who had been at the party from which Colleen disappeared. She went on to say he showed a sexual interest in her sister, but Colleen turned him down. Jay Hart was allegedly also present at the party in which four-year-old Evelyn disappeared. Evelyn's mother admitted after Hart's arrest that he tried to have sex with her that night too, but she also turned him down. She blacked out toward the end of the night after consuming a large amount of alcohol. When she had woken in the morning, she found her shorts and underwear around her ankles. This event paled in comparison to finding her daughter missing minutes later, so she never mentioned it to anyone. The pieces were now starting to fall into place, though, and soon, a substantial part of the puzzle would emerge.

Another Body

Just 19 days after Jay Hart's arrest for the murder of Clinton Speedy-Duroux, as he languished in jail awaiting trial for that crime, another set of remains were discovered just a few yards from where Clinton's body was. These remains, however, were far more skeletonized, and the small size of the bones left the police were confident they had finally found four-year-old Evelyn Greenup.

Although Evelyn's body was in no condition for an autopsy, a hole in her skull was remarkably similar to the injury sustained by Clinton Speedy-Duroux. A sharp implement had been driven through the child's skull and into her brain. There were similarities in the causes of death, pointing to Jay Hart again, police charged Hart with Evelyn's murder on the 16th of October 1991. Unfortunately, there was insufficient evidence to prove that he had involvement in her death without Colleen's remains. Hence, the family had to hedge their bets that they would receive justice, by default, through the trial for the two other murders.

The Trial

The murder trial against Jay Hart for the murder of 16-year-old Clinton Speedy-Duroux would last almost two years. The evidence against Hart, however, was mostly circumstantial. Police had been so slow to react, giving Hart more than sufficient time to destroy any physical evidence that could link him to Clinton, assuming such evidence existed.

Prosecutors attempted to have both Clinton and Evelyn's murder heard in the same trial as, they argued, the chance that Hart would innocently implicate in both crimes was very slim. They hoped to use the similarities between the incidents to make up for the lack of physical evidence. The judge refused to allow this and ruled the trials for each murder were to be held separately. This ruling hugely impeded the prosecution's case against Hart, and the obstacle proved to be impossible when, in February 1994, the judge acquitted Hart of Clinton's murder. After this acquittal, the prosecution decided to withdraw the charges for Evelyn's death and, instead, continued to investigate in hopes that new evidence would emerge.

Double Jeopardy

The prosecution decided not to proceed with the trial for Evelyn's murder because of a legal policy in effect in New South Wales called double jeopardy. At the time of the crimes, the double jeopardy policy prevented prosecutors from retrying the same person twice for the same crime regardless of whether new evidence emerged that proved the accused's guilt.

In 2006, this law would be slightly relaxed to allow for new trials against the same accused only in murder cases and also only if discovering entirely new and compelling evidence.

Justice for Evelyn

In 2004, after a significant reinvestigation into Evelyn Greenup's murder, and having two alleged confessions Hart made to the crime, Jay Hart was again placed under arrest, charged and put on trial, this time for the murder of Evelyn Greenup. Sadly, despite a monumental effort by prosecutors, he was acquitted of this murder in 2006.

In the same year, however, the relaxation in the double jeopardy laws came into effect, and this gave hope to Evelyn's family that justice may not be impossible. What they would have to find, though, was brand new, compelling evidence. As there was no possibility of finding new physical evidence at this point, the prosecution felt their last chance might be to draw the connection disallowed in the first trial for Clinton's murder. While, at that time, the judge ruled the "*similar fact*" evidence to be inadmissible. The laws around evidence admissibility also changed, creating some hope for the prosecutors to use that change to their benefit. In 2016, the possibility was dismissed by an Australian court, dashing any hope for the Greenups' in finding justice for Evelyn. This turn of events, unfortunately, also means that prosecution will not be able to use "*similar fact*" evidence to try Hart for Colleen Walker-Craig's murder.

As of 2018, the prosecution has explored further avenues to broaden the definition of "new and compelling" to present evidence the courts would previously have deemed inadmissible. However, even if granted, there is no guarantee that new trials for any of the three murders would result in a guilty verdict.

(*Hamer, 2018*).

The Australian legal system does not have a jury, and it is a judge alone who decides a guilty or not guilty verdict. In some respects, this makes certain cases easier to try, but in other cases, such as the Bowraville murders, it may be a stumbling block. It may be more suitable for a jury of laypeople to accept the circumstantial evidence presented than for a legally trained judge.

Is Jay Hart a Serial Killer?

While the circumstantial evidence against Jay Hart is, at least to a layperson, compelling, many believe that he is an innocent victim of a police force. He needed to find someone to take the rap for their ineptitude. Hart only offered an alibi for one of the murders, and that was for Clinton's case. Jay claimed he and Clinton left the party together at around 3 am, but by 6 am, he was at work, which was confirmed. That meant he would have less than three hours to kill Clinton and dispose of his body before reporting for his shift at 6 am. Dan Box, the journalist who produced and hosted the investigative podcast, *Bowraville*, went out to the site in 2016 to try to recreate the events and see if Jay would indeed have had enough time to carry out the crime.

Jay said he set his alarm for 05:15 am that morning, but when he awoke, he felt so ill from drinking the night before that he fell asleep again. He claimed, though, that before he had fallen back to sleep, Jay heard someone, who he assumed to be Clinton, leave the caravan. Then claimed when he woke up again, it was a few minutes before 6 am. Jay said Clinton was not in the trailer at that point, and he rushed into the house, not wanting to be late for work.

Jay ordinarily had a friend pick him up for work, but that morning, he believed that he must have missed his lift, so instead, he took his mother's car and drove toward his work site. Jay then saw his friend pulling into his road and turned around and went back. He told his friend he wanted to have a cup of tea and then head off to work, and he would just use his mother's car to get there. In spite, Jay making it clear at the beginning of his statement, he wanted to avoid being late for work. It would have already been past 6 am at that time. Interestingly, the friend reported that when he arrived at the caravan to collect Jay, he heard an alarm clock inside the trailer. If Jay switched it off as he claimed, it would not have still been going off.

(Bowraville Podcast, 2016).

The possibility remains, though, when Jay returned to the caravan that day and met his friend, he did not return from a short trip halfway to work but rather from a much longer journey, during which he dumped Clinton's body. He suddenly decided to stay for "a cup of tea" rather than make it to work on time because he needed to clean the caravan of any remaining evidence. Clinton's girlfriend, however, found evidence he had been at the trailer that night. The sneakers Clinton never went anywhere without were in the caravan, making Jay's story of hearing Clinton leave the trailer around 5:15 am rather unlikely since Clinton wouldn't have left without his shoes.

Also stated in the podcast was a witness who testified he saw Jay's mother's vehicle leaving the residence much earlier than 6 am. But, he hadn't been able to identify who was driving. Other witnesses cast further doubt on Jay's guilt by saying they saw a male hitchhiker, who resembled Clinton, in various places around Bowraville that day after 6 am.

Witnesses claimed to have seen 4-year-old Evelyn walking around town on her own the day after she disappeared from the party. The only link prosecutors had to bind Jay to Evelyn's murder was the fact that she was allegedly never seen alive again after the party he attended. If these multiple witnesses were right as to what they saw, Evelyn might not have gone missing that night. Of course, it is also possible the girl seen was another young Aboriginal girl of Evelyn's age, but the possibility remains that it was her. Years later, when reinterviewed, it turned out that many of these witnesses were not in Bowraville on the day in question, and still others say they weren't sure it was Evelyn they saw. Unfortunately, their evidence had already done its damage in court.

Jay's family doesn't believe he was capable of committing these murders, and they argue that surely if the evidence were so significant, they would have convicted Jay by now. Four prisoners would come forward to say Jay confessed to them that he killed Clinton, but testimony from convicts are in most cases, assumed that they would be getting some form of reward for their statement. As the years go on, memories fade, and specific aspects of testimony change and become unreliable

(Bowraville Podcast, 2016).

At this point, it is highly unlikely Jay Hart, or anyone else, will be found guilty of the three child murders in Bowraville unless a conscience starts to weigh too heavily or someone gives a deathbed confession. The question remains, is Jay Hart, a serial killer, and if he isn't, who is?

Three Lost Souls

Jay Hart is now 54 years old. He no longer lives in Bowraville, but the town he does now live in has accepted him as one of their own. His neighbors speak highly of him and say he is a great father and grandfather, and he has never caused them a day of worry as a neighbor or resident. Jay's neighbors from his Bowraville days, of course, had a very different picture of him. As far as records show, Jay Hart has not been a suspect or convicted of any further crimes since the Bowraville murders. Jay Hart still insists that he is innocent. A court of law, on several occasions, has not found sufficient evidence to prove his guilt.

Toward the end of the podcast, the host speaks to a woman who was Jay Hart's past partner and also the aunt of Colleen Walker-Craig. She mentions that if the law of Australia won't get the person who killed these three children. Then Aboriginal law will, referring to the mystical belief that if the Aboriginal community holds onto their need for justice, then the perpetrator of a crime, whether they are in jail or not, will be unable to rest. The person who is responsible for these three heinous crimes, she believes, will be driven mad by their guilt. It's a pleasant thought and akin to the idea we have of "karma," but one must ask if that is enough.

Colleen Walker-Craig, Evelyn Greenup, and Clinton Speedy-Duroux lost their lives in a horrific and senseless manner, and the person who committed those crimes, whether it was Jay Hart or not, is still walking free. Is it enough that they have to live with their guilt or be driven mad by some mystical force of karma? For those of us who believe in punitive justice, it is certainly not good enough, but 30 years later, those three souls are still gone, and a fourth wanders the earth holding on to his secret.

CHAPTER 3

THE MAN IN THE BAG

P olice place caution tape around the perimeter of the apartment, a foul smell permeated the air. It was 11:30 AM on Monday, the 23rd of August 2010. A desperate woman made a phone call to her brother's employer.

She had not been able to make contact with her brother, Gareth Williams, and his place of work confirmed they had also not seen him in days. She requested that they inform the police and require a welfare check, and at 4:40 that afternoon, police made entry into a top floor apartment in Alderney Street, Pimlico, a district of London. As officers entered the flat, a wave of heat hit them. It was a lovely summer day in London with temperatures peaking around 23 degrees Celsius (*74 degrees Fahrenheit*), so there was no need for the heating to be on in this upper-level apartment that received ample sun through its large windows. Then, the smell started to creep into the officers' nostrils. Those who have ever been around a dead body will tell you that there is no mistaking the stench of human decomposition. The officers methodically made their way through the apartment, eventually discovering the smell in the otherwise spotless bathroom. Inside the bathtub was a large North Face brand sports bag sealed with a padlock, but decomposition fluid began to leak through the seams and fabric, and there was no doubt in the police officers' minds what they would find when they opened the bag. The question remained, though, was the corpse in the bag their missing person, or was it someone else?

The Man in the Bag

Investigators shut down the crime scene, and the forensic team gradually made their way into the duffle bag. The severely decomposed body of 31-year-old Gareth Williams was inside. As forensic investigators carefully lifted the remains out of the duffle bag, they found another strange clue underneath the body — the key to the padlock that sealed the bag. No DNA, fingerprints, or palm prints would be found on the bag or the rim of the bath — not even from Gareth himself. In the living room, officers found Gareth's laptop, mobile phone, and other personal items laid out neatly on a table. None of the articles had any fingerprints or DNA on them. An officer who was at the scene would later say that it was like everything had been laid out for them to find.

As police launched an investigation into this strange death, circumstances would get even more bizarre when they looked into Gareth Williams' occupation. Gareth was initially from Anglesey in Wales. He was brilliant and received his first degree from Bangor University at the age of 17. While working on his Ph.D. at the University of Manchester, the Government Communication Headquarters (*GCHQ*) recruited Gareth.

Through the GCHQ, they appointed him to MI6 (*the British Secret Intelligence Service*). Although much of Gareth's work involved high-level data analysis, he is alleged to have carried out some fieldwork during his time with MI6, Gareth Williams was mainly a spy.

(*People's Tonight, 2018*)

As London police discovered this, they realized that this investigation was going to be very different from most others conducted. Gareth's family, though, were like every other grieving family. They wanted answers and justice for their loved one, regardless of his occupation. The lack of any evidence found on or around the bag made the family suspicious, and they would go on to say, *"they believed the police either messed up the investigation by damaging evidence or purposefully removed crucial proof as part of a cover-up..."*

An autopsy determined that Gareth had been dead for at least ten days, and the advanced state of decomposition made it very difficult to decide on a cause of death. It also resulted in skewed toxicology results, so if Gareth had ingested some sort of poison, it would be nearly impossible to identify.

A Strange Investigation

From the outset, police blocked any information from releasing to the public, so conspiracy theories started up almost immediately. Gareth's family could not understand why the GCHQ or MI6 had not reported Gareth as missing when he had not arrived for work for ten days. They wanted to know why the GCHQ only contacted the police at 4:30 on the day they found Gareth's body while his sister called them at 11:30. GCHQ declined to offer comment on either of these points.

There was also a lot of information withheld from the police about Gareth's work. They were not even allowed to interview his colleagues and had to rely on anonymous statements provided by MI6. The detective inspector in charge of the case didn't even know about eight USB drives that had been found in Gareth's office until 18 months into the investigation. Presumably, GCHQ and MI6 had first scanned these drives themselves for any sensitive information before handing them over to the police.

Working with the information they did have access to, police would soon announce that Gareth Williams was known to have a keen interest in bondage. This so-called keen interest was only demonstrated by an occasional visit, over several months, to websites that presented the content. This find seemed to convince investigators that Gareth's death had somehow been a sex game gone wrong. They alleged that he visited drag clubs, and they found a significant amount of high-end women's clothing in his home, which, they claimed, meant that Gareth was interested in cross-dressing. Many people, including his family, did not believe that his sexual interests had anything to do with his death.

The Inquest

Due to the significant lack of movement in the case, an inquest was held into Gareth's death to determine whether there was substantial evidence for his murder. One of the most important questions asked at this inquest was whether Gareth could have locked himself in the bag. Besides the sex game possibility, the suggestion also tabled Gareth to practice his escape skills and found himself trapped. A pathologist for the Home Office claimed that this was indeed possible. Still, an expert in rescue from confined spaces testified, stating he had purchased a bag identical to the one Gareth was found in and had attempted to trap himself inside the bag in the same manner. Out of the 400 attempts he made at replicating the scene. The expert had been unsuccessful at locking himself in the bag on all occasions. But he also stated it would be difficult to arrange a corpse in the position Williams was. It's more likely Williams was alive when he got into the duffle bag.

The inquest, which concluded in 2012, permanently left everyone with more questions than answers. Although the coroner in charge of the investigation would not make an absolute determination, she couldn't rule out that Gareth's death was accidental. Due to a lack of evidence to the contrary, the inquest would uphold this as the predominant finding. In 2013, the police would also announce that they also believed Gareth's death was an accident. However, the family and a large portion of the interested public were unconvinced.

(*Warren, 2017*).

One of the reasons the police accepted the accident theory was because of Gareth's previous landladies. The woman claimed that in 2007, she and her husband found Gareth tied to his bed and shouting for help. Gareth claimed he tied himself to the bed to see if he could free himself but had been unable to.

The theory that Gareth's death was a homicide related to his work as a codebreaker for MI6 strengthened. The investigators later revealed that Gareth started working with the US National Security Agency in an operation that would help to bring down a money-laundering scheme run by the Russian mafia.

The Russian Connection

In 2015, a former Russian Komitet Gosudarstvennoy Bezopasnosti (*KGB*) agent defected to the United States and revealed his belief the Russian Foreign Intelligence Services had assassinated Gareth Williams. He claimed that the manner of death was an untraceable poison injected into Gareth's ear. This injection site, along with the advanced decomposition, made it impossible to confirm or deny this claim. Gareth was also allegedly approached by someone asking him to become a double agent for the Russians. Gareth refused, but since he knew the double agent's identity, Gareth needed to be silenced.

(*People's Tonight, 2018*).

When revealing this link, a media outlet called *Buzzfeed* launched an in-depth investigation into the Russian connection. This investigation revealed the US and UK Secret Services were conducting a joint operation into the deaths of 13 other people believed to have been assassinated by Russian agents. In all 13 deaths, police investigators had ruled out homicide, but behind the scenes, this secret joint team was investigating the deaths more closely.

The victims of this alleged plot include:

- Johnny Elichaoff, who died on 1 November 2014

- Robby Curtis, who died on 1 December 2012

- Paul Castle, who died on 17 December 2010

- Stephen Curtis, who died on 3 March 2004

- Boris Berezovsky, who died on 23 March 2013

- Scot Young, who died on 8 December 2014

- Igor Ponomarev, who died on 30 October 2006

- Alexander Litvinenko, who died on 23 November 2006

- Alexander Perepilichnyy, who died on 10 November 2012

- Daniel McGrory, who died on 20 February 2007

- Matthew Puncher, who died on 4 May 2016

- Badri Patarkatsishvili, who died on 12 February 2008

- Yuri Golubev, who died on 7 January 2007

- Stephen Moss, who died on 22 September 2003

All of these men could be linked together somehow, and they all had links back to Gareth Williams. All these men had some connection to the Russian mafia, the Kremlin, or Russian Secret Security, whether in their work (*some were journalists*) or through nefarious dealings. The causes of death in each of these incidents was such that it did not immediately point to murder, but the circumstances were highly suspicious.

Accident or Murder?

While undoubtedly, this intriguing case is full of mystery and many rabbit holes, it is essential for us never to forget that Gareth Williams was a human being. Gareth's work nor his interest defined him. He was someone's son and someone's brother, and, if his death is indeed foul play, he deserves justice just as much as any other murder victim. Will his family ever know the truth about what happened to Gareth? In all honesty, this seems unlikely. If even the police were restricted from receiving much of the information about his case, it is highly improbable that the public will ever know the truth.

The scenario that Gareth somehow locked himself inside the bag seems highly unlikely, if not impossible. The logistics of placing yourself inside a duffle bag and then being able to secure a padlock from the inside without damaging it does not add up in anyone's mind. The fact that the key was inside the bag with Gareth's body could be viewed in one of two ways. It could further prove the idea that Gareth was practicing his escape skills. It could have also been a sick joke or a red herring by the perpetrator to make police think Gareth put himself in the bag. The lack of any DNA or fingerprints on the duffle bag, bath, and Gareth's belongings is bizarre. At the very least, you would expect to have found his prints on the lock if he put himself in the bag.

While many may feel that the Russian connection is simply conspiracy theory, we would be remiss to dismiss it. Such underground operations do exist. These conspiracies are the very reason that we have secret service and intelligence agencies in countries across the world. Agents that work for such bureaus understand that even if they are not doing fieldwork, there is a significant risk to their safety. Gareth Williams was a precious asset to the British secret service, and his skills at codebreaking would have been in high demand. It is not too far of a stretch to believe that the Russian secret service could have tried to turn Gareth into a double agent.

If we look solely at physical and circumstantial evidence, there seems to be far more evidence to point to someone else's involvement in the death of Gareth Williams. The fact remains, though, we will likely never know the truth, and we can only hope that if rumors of covert involvement are accurate, these forces are being dealt with to the harshest extent possible.

CHAPTER 4

BODY IN THE CHURCHYARD!

On the morning, 8th of June 1992, a woman was walking through the churchyard at St. Joseph's church in Zaandam, North-Holland. A large pond flanked the churchyard, and as the woman made her way to work, she chose to walk on the grass verge between the concrete churchyard and the pond. She spotted a shoe and then what appeared to be blood on the grass leading into the pond. Concerned that some-one may have injured themselves and fallen into the fishpond, the woman ran into the church and alerted the pastor. Both ran out to take a closer look at the patch of water around the bloodstain and shoe but could not see a person.

The pastor promised to alert the police, and the woman continued on her way. From his home, located next to the church, the pastor had a different view of the pond, including a section covered in thick reeds. As he entered his house to make the promised phone call to authorities, he looked out the window and saw the partially nude, deceased body of a young female in the reeds.

No More Buses

Milica van Doorn was a beautiful 19-year-old blond teenager who'd recently finished her final year of high school. Milica was waiting for her exam results to see if she could continue to her tertiary qualification to achieve her dream of becoming a teacher. Milica was the middle of three sisters and lived with her parents in Zaandam, a town in North Holland, situated on the banks of the Zaan river region.

On the evening of Sunday the 7th of June 1992, Milica left her parents' home to attend a birthday party at her friends' apartment. The apartment, located on Fluiterkruit Road in the Kogerveld District of Zaandam, was just a short bus ride away from her house. While at the party, Milica asked the friend about the bus schedule that night, as she was likely planning in advance what time she would need to leave to catch the bus back home. Her friend told Milica that the buses ran every half hour without fail. Around midnight, she said goodbye to her friends and walked to the bus stop, which was 200 yards away from the apartment building.

When she arrived, however, Milica realized her friend had not taken into account the celebration of the religious festival of the Pentecost was that weekend. Therefore, the bus schedule had changed, and the last bus for the night left at 11:24 pm. Unperturbed, Milica decided to walk to the train station. The last people to see Milica were a couple who were walking in the opposite direction that night. The next person to see her, besides her killer, was the pastor who found her body.

(*Teller Report, 2018*).

Savage

Milica van Doorn received savage injuries to her body. There were several deep stab wounds to her neck, and her throat had been slit. She was also raped. Forensic analysts were able to retrieve a sample of male DNA and pubic hair from Milica's body. The Netherlands reeled with shock at the news of this vicious attack, and police started an intensive investigation to bring Milica's killer to justice.

Just days after pulling her body from the churchyard pond, Milica's family received her final year school results in the mail. She passed her exams with flying colors and would have easily qualified to start studying to be a teacher. Sadly, that dream was now gone forever.

Authorities questioned the couple which last saw Milica on the street on the night of her murder. They mentioned having seen a man who appeared to be of Turkish descent riding a bicycle in the area. They remembered the man because he had been singing and came up behind them on the bike and then passed them as Milica was walking in the opposite direction. They said the man turned around and headed back in the path that Milica was walking. They eventually lost sight of both of them. Unfortunately, police were not able to identify the man on the bicycle, and Milica's case would soon become cold.

DNA

Although the possibility of identifying individuals through DNA first emerged in the 1980s, it took many years to develop sophisticated techniques to be used as evidence in a court of law. The initial DNA testing methods also required large samples, and any testing done on smaller samples ran the risk of using up the specimen entirely and leaving nothing for future testing when technology improved. For this reason, many homicide investigators across the world who investigated cases in the 1990s and early 2000s would often hold off on performing DNA tests if they ran the risk of using the sample entirely. It was predominantly this reason that the first DNA tests performed on the semen sample found on Milica's body were in 2001. Investigators compared the DNA profile to the person of interest they identified in their original investigation, as well as all of the males in the Kogerveld area with criminal records. This search yielded no match. In 2004, another screening of the local male population was done, which, again, yielded no positive results.

In 2008, DNA technology advanced to such a degree that it was possible to determine the offender's geographic region of origin through their DNA sample. The forensic examiner tested the sample from Milica's killer and concluded that the man was of Turkish or North African descent. This evidence tied in perfectly with the eyewitness account from the couple regarding the singing man on the bicycle. A total of 75 men with Turkish ancestry who lived in the Kogerveld area in 1992 were contacted and asked to submit a DNA sample for testing voluntarily.

Unfortunately, this round of testing was also unsuccessful in identifying a perpetrator. At this time, familial or ancestral DNA was becoming a commonly used tool in investigations across the world, and the public called for this to be used in Milica's case. Familial DNA tests a broader pool of donors by checking for ancestral DNA connections. This type of testing helps to identify the perpetrator's brothers, cousins, nephews, and nephews rather than just the one profile, therefore widening the net significantly. Unfortunately, in 2008, the law in the

Netherlands still prohibited such testing for criminal cases, seeing it as invasive of personal privacy.

It would take another eight years before familial DNA research was made legal in the country and another 18 months until a new DNA search could start. The examiner collected DNA from 133 men with Turkish ancestry, who lived in the Kogerveld area in 1992 and handed it over to the Netherlands Forensic Institute for familial DNA testing. On the 9th of December 2017, the NFI contacted the investigating officers on Milica van Doorn's case and advised them that they managed to identify the brother of the offender that left the DNA sample on Milica's body.

On the 9th of December, a man matching the DNA sample, who at the time of the latest news updates, identified as "Hüseyin A." was arrested. Hüseyin was living just a few hundred yards from where Milica's body was. In the years since Milica's murder, Hüseyin married and had four children. There was no link to any other similar crimes in the area. Hüseyin's lawyer would later claim that his client believed he was possessed the night of Milica's murder.

Is This Justice?

In December 2018, Hüseyin was found guilty of the murder of Milica van Doorn. He could not be charged or tried for her rape as the statute of limitations for rape in the Netherlands had expired. The judge sentenced Hüseyin to 20-years in prison, which was what the prosecutor requested. Given that he was 47 years old when incarcerated, he will only be 67 when he is released.

(*Pieters, 2018*).

Whether this sentence truly represents justice or not is perhaps a matter of personal opinion. Milica did not get the opportunity to study to be a teacher as she wanted to or have children of her own. Hüseyin, on the other hand, had 26 years on the outside after brutally raping and killing her to build a life, have children, and enjoy the fruits of his labor. When he gets out of jail, he will still be young enough to enjoy his children and grandchildren.

For 26 years, he lived just a few hundred yards from the churchyard where he raped and murdered Milica and the pond where he dumped her body. What was going through his mind in those two and a half decades? Did he attend that church? Did he let his children play on the banks of the pond that once been his killing ground? The question remains: Did Hüseyin not commit another crime in those 26 years? Is it possible that someone who so viciously murdered a young woman when he was just 21 could actually go on with the rest of his life and never feel that urge again?

Hüseyin never gave his version of the events that night, so Milica's family still does not know what her last minutes were like; they will likely never know. Milica van Doorn was walking on the sidewalk, minding her own business, and trying to get home. Did she hear the singing man come up behind her? Was the last thing she listened to the song of a madman?

CHAPTER 5

SERIAL KILLING COUPLE

The smell of diesel fuel flowed through the air as two roaring excavators rolled down a beautiful suburban street. Cromwell Street was like any other suburban street in Gloucester, England, up until the excavation equipment rolled up to house number 25 in February 1994. The residents of the home, the West family, had seemed rather ordinary to their neighbors. The matriarch of the household, Rose, was known to have a bit of a temper, and it hadn't been uncommon for her neighbors to hear her voice echo angrily down the street. She certainly wasn't the only frustrated housewife in Gloucester.

As the excavators began their work, and chunks of ground uplifted, the secrets the West family had been hiding would reveal something sinister, and their neighbors would realize what horrors went on right next door. By the time Gloucester police finished at 25 Cromwell Street, they would unearth ten bodies, and police would find another two nearby, introducing the world to one of the deadliest serial killer couples of all time.

Fred: Deadly Beginnings

The instability in Fred West's family could be traced back to several generations. The two people who were the most significant influence in his early life were his parents Walter and Daisy West. Daisy West gave birth to her son Frederick on the 29th of September 1941, and she was immediately in awe of her curly, dark-haired child. Allegedly Frederick was by far the favorite, in his mother's eyes, among all of his five siblings. But, this connection had a dark side with allegations of his mother sexually abusing him from a young age.

Much of what we know about Fred's parents have come either from Fred himself or from his siblings, which means it may not be accurate, but there is very little doubt the first West household was far from ordinary.

Allegedly Fred's father would rape his daughters regularly, as well as the daughters of his neighbors. He raised Fred to believe that sex was his birthright as a man, and if he wanted something, he should just take it. Many of Fred's childhood neighbors described him as a "normal, lovely" young man and said that although he was a little cheeky, that was no different from many of the other teenagers in the Herefordshire village in which they lived.

Fred was not academically inclined, and he left school at the age of 17 to become a laborer. Soon after, he would incur two separate head injuries and have a metal plate inserted into his head. Experts have since speculated that these injuries could have altered his impulse control and emotional awareness. There may be some truth to this claim as it was shortly after having recovered from his operation to insert the metal plate Fred began to get into trouble.

Before giving him too much leeway for his behavior, it's important to say. Most career criminals will start committing crimes around the same age Fred did. He already displayed lewd sexual behavior before these injuries, so he was undoubtedly already primed for the criminal role he was about to take on. His first brush with the law for a sexual offense occurred when he was 20 years old, where Fred impregnated a 13-year-old girl in his town. Strangely, despite his family's reported free-thinking around sex, Fred was shunned by his family for this act and kicked out of the family home. One can only wonder if his parents were angry about what he did or mad he got caught and may bring the authorities' focus on their acts?

At this point, Fred became a construction worker and lived on his own. But his trouble with the law wouldn't end there. He was regularly fired for stealing from his employers and had several minors accuse him of rape and molestation. One of these cases made it to court, but the court ruled Fred's actions to be affected by his brain injuries, and they found him guilty of just the molestation charges. So Fred did not have to go to jail. This event is one of the many that Fred should've gone to prison for good, but managed to sidestep the law.

In 1962, Fred married his first wife, Rena Costello, a Scottish woman with a criminal record for theft and prostitution. At the time, Rena was pregnant but not with Fred's child. He seemed to have little issue with this, though, and in 1963, Rena gave birth to a baby girl named Charmaine. The following year, she gave birth to Fred's child, also a girl named Anna Marie.

Anna McFall also came into Fred and Rena's life at this time. Anna McFall became friends with the couple and acted as a nanny to the children. When Fred and Rena decided to move to Gloucester, Anna Mcfall moved with them. The predominant reason behind their move was that Fred found a new job at a slaughterhouse in Gloucester.

The couples moved into the new town and would coincide with eight sexual assaults. The perpetrator's description of these assaults matched Fred, but the link to him wasn't made immediately. Rena and Fred's marriage deteriorated quite quickly, and she soon returned to Scotland, leaving Charmaine and Anna Marie behind with Fred and Anna McFall. After Rena's departure, Fred and Anna McFall became partners, and she was soon pregnant with his child. She, however, made the mistake of insisting that he divorce Rena and marry her instead. In July 1967, Fred West murdered Anna McFall and her unborn child. He mutilated her corpse in a manner that would become a signature for him by removing her fingers and toes before burying her near the caravan park in which he lived. Rena then returned to live with Fred briefly.

In January 1968, a 15-year-old girl, Mary Bastholm, went missing from a bus stop in Gloucester. Circumstantial evidence would later link Fred to this abduction and possible murder, but prosecutors could not build a case to convict him. In November 1968, he met the woman that would join him on his murderous journey.

Rose: Deadly Beginnings

Rosemary Letts' parents both had a mental illness. Doctors diagnosed her father with paranoid schizophrenia, and her mother suffered from severe depression and received regular electroconvulsive therapy (*ECT*) treatments. Little's known about the effects of ECT on pregnant women in 1953, but one week before Daisy

Letts gave birth to Rosemary, she was still receiving ECT. When Rosemary was born, the effects of the ECT on her were apparent. She would rhythmically rock her head until she was in a trance state, and her siblings complained that she continuously knocked her head against her cot at night. As she grew, it became clear that she had very little control over her impulses and would fly into a rage at school and home.

Besides the physical obstacles of her childhood, she also struggled with her violent and abusive father and her cold and distant mother. Her mother allegedly fallen into a deep depression and withdrew entirely from her family. Her father started to assault his daughters sexually. Rose became attached to her abuser, likely knowing that the best way to appease him was to be like him. Her younger brothers would later allege that when Rose was 13, she started to abuse them sexually. She also had an obsession with older men and was highly sexualized at a very young age.

Daisy Letts would leave her husband when Rose was a teenager and took her children with her, but Rose chose to return to live with her father shortly afterward. Soon after moving back in with her father, at 15 years old, Rose met a young man named Fred West, 12 years senior. Rose's father strongly objected to the relationship from the outset, but the girl was utterly enamored with this older man who shared many of the same sexual interests she did.

Rose and Fred were so similar in so many ways that they simply seemed a match made in hell. Within months, Rose moved in with Fred, and she began caring for his step-daughter Charmaine, who was six at the time, and his daughter, Anna Marie, then five years old. The girls' mother Rena Costello was still in and out of their lives and would occasionally visit them but spent most of her time in Scotland. By 1968, when Rose was 16 years old, she fell pregnant with Fred's child. In 1970, she gave birth to the couple's first daughter together, Heather.

(Bray, 2019)

Rose's First Murder

Domestic bliss was not to be, though, as Fred, found guilty of several theft charges, failed to pay fines for other offenses, and was sent to jail. Rose, at 17 years old, was left to care for three small children on her own. Fred was abusing both older girls, and as soon as he went to jail, Rose quickly slipped into his role as a tormentor. She allegedly forced the girls to undress and then tie them to their beds for long periods, during which they were not allowed to move or speak. She would also gag them so they couldn't scream and then beat them across the legs with a leather whip. Although we may never know the exact details of what took place next, it seems that one of these beatings went too far. While Fred was still in prison, Rose killed Charmaine, then just eight years old. Although Rose would later claim she knew nothing of Fred's previous murders and crimes, what she did next casts doubt on that. Instead of fleeing in fear of her partner's wrath when he returned from prison and found his oldest child dead, Rose stayed where she was and kept the body hidden in the basement. Pointing to the fact that Rose was well aware of Fred's prior deeds, and he would have no choice but to help her get rid of Charmaine's body.

Further proof of this couple's complicity in murder is after having been released from jail and having to bury his daughter's body, Fred married Rose in 1972, legally sealing their poisonous connection. Charmaine's body would not stay buried, and it is a known fact that Fred dug up the child's body and reburied it, at least once, and removed her fingers and toes, which became his signature act. It seemed inevitable to the couple that when Charmaine's mother Rena would come to visit, she would have to die, and this is what happened. As soon as Rena arrived at the house and asked where Charmaine was, Fred strangled her, removed her fingers and toes, and buried her in the same area where he had buried Anna McFall's body.

The couple cruelly told Seven-year-old Anna Marie her mother had come to fetch Charmaine to live in Scotland and left her behind. She would not be returning to see her again. The cruelty level of this couple seems to know no bounds. Not only were they sexually, emotionally, and physically abusing this child. But they then saw fit, after murdering her mother and sister, to further traumatize her by telling her that her mother chose her sister over her, abandoning her. All done to protect themselves, so that little Anna Marie did not ask questions or talk outside the house. They likely made Anna Marie feel ashamed for being abandoned, so the child would not tell anyone her mother allegedly left her behind.

The Cromwell Street Years

In 1972, shortly after getting married, the West family moved to what would become their infamous Cromwell Street address, also welcoming another daughter into the world - Mae. The idea behind moving to a larger house was to be able to take in lodgers to supplement their income. Rose was operating as a sex worker on and off at Fred's instruction, but she would not always charge for her services and simply brought men and women into the house to have sexual encounters with while Fred watched. Fred found it extremely difficult to hold down a job, so often, Rose's sex work income and the money from the lodgers were the only money coming into the West household.

The main appeal of the house at 25 Cromwell Street was the large basement, which Fred setup as a torture chamber soon after they moved in. The first victim to be assaulted, beaten, raped, and strung from the ceiling was Fred's daughter, Anna Marie. In 1972, the basement saw its first outside victim when the couple hired Caroline Owens as a nanny. The 17-year-old barely worked for the West family for a few days when she was taken down to the basement, raped, and tortured. Caroline would later say, Fred told her they were going to kill her and bury her in the basement, but she was able to escape through a window and reported the incident to the police.

Rose was pregnant again at this time, and, amazingly, the couple convinced the court that the acts were consensual, and they merely received fines for their actions. Caroline Owens, who was terrified to be in the same room as the West couple, did not testify, which is likely the reason for this ruling.

Then the couple would have their first son, Stephen, who was born in August 1972. This last brush with the law seemed to have had an impact on the West's because they seemingly decided to ensure that no further victims would leave their basement alive. The following women would all fall victim to Fred and Rose over the coming years. They were brutally assaulted and murdered. Their dismembered remains were all buried at 25 Cromwell Street, predominantly in the basement:

- Lynda Gough

- Juanita Mott

- Alison Chambers

- Lucy Partington

- Therese Siegenthaler

- Shirley Hubbard

- Carol Ann Cooper

- Shirley Robinson

Rose West would give birth to several more children at Cromwell Street, although authorities believe not all were fathered by Fred. He had no problem with Rose performing sex work or engaging in sex acts with other men as long as he could watch. The West family would soon include another son, Barry, and daughters Louise, Lucyanna, Rosemary Junior, and Tara. The last three girls believed to have been born of relations between Rose and one of her sex work clients. The children were, to a certain extent, aware of their parents' activities, but they were threatened with violence if they ever spoke outside of the family.

Anna Marie left home to live with her boyfriend. She had been their primary sexual target out of the girls. Heather was next in line for the abuse from her father. Heather was far less compliant than her sister, though, and soon confessed to what was happening to a friend. When Fred and Rosemary became aware of this, they killed Heather and buried her in the garden of 25 Cromwell Street. They allegedly made their son Stephen dig his sister's grave.

Secrets Revealed

Although Fred and Rose did their best to ensure that no more victims escaped, several did, and in 1992 after another of these victims reported their assault, Constable Hazel Savage was able to secure a search warrant for 25 Cromwell Street. She found various items of pornography and proof of child abuse in the home. Fred and Rose were both arrested on rape and sodomy charges. Police interviewed the West children, and Anna Marie revealed that Charmaine and Heather both disappeared. Anna Marie admitted that, at times, her parents would threaten them by saying if they didn't behave, they would end up *"under the patio like Heather."* Police removed the younger children from the residence, Rose and Fred's cruel house of cards was quickly starting to crumble. Rose let out on bail attempted to commit suicide. Her son found her just in time, and she survived.

The rape and sodomy cases against the West soon started to falter as Rose, now living among her older children again, began to threaten them, and they, in turn, stopped cooperating with police. Constable Savage pressed on, though, and in February 1994, the police began to dig up the premises at 25 Cromwell Street. They initially only found two bodies, one of Shirley Robinson and the other, Heather West.

In a strange twist, Fred would be the one to reveal to police that nine more bodies he buried in the basement of the house. It is entirely possible that if Fred had not told police about these bodies, they would still lay buried there to this day. Rose, on the other hand, denied all knowledge of any of the murders. She claimed that Fred solely committed the atrocities that took place. Fred continued to cooperate with police, and also told them where to find their first three victims.

The Trial

On the 13th of December 1994, Fred West was charged with 12 counts of murder and remanded to Winson Green Prison. On the 1st of January 1995, he decided to leave Rose to face justice on her own and take the rest of his secrets with him as he tied a bedsheet around his neck and hung himself until he was dead.

International media coverage of Rose's trial exploded as the public had to come to terms with the fact that Rose was equally involved in the murders and was not an innocent victim, as she claimed. She would eventually be found guilty of 10 of the killings, and although initially, given a 25-year sentence, she soon changed to a "whole life tariff," which means she will die in jail. Rose refused to accept her sentence and launched two appeals, both of which were unsuccessful.

(*Biography*, 2019).

The Aftermath

The city completely demolished the house at 25 Cromwell Street and was replaced with a pathway leading to the Gloucester town center. The West children, understandably, struggled to adjust to the knowledge that they lived in a house of horrors, and it would take a long time for them to free from the psychological grip their mother still held over them. In the years following her mother's conviction, Mae West wrote a book detailing her horrific childhood called, *Love, As Always, Mum*. The book reveals letters her mother wrote from jail and intimate secrets about the hell that was her life with her parents. She also admitted she was raped by her uncle from the age of five, suggesting that her family's degradation went far beyond the Cromwell Street residents. Mae West now lives under a different name in an undisclosed English town. She told reporters she was terrified of revealing her identity and victimizing her family because of the connection to her parents.

Lucyanna Mae intended not to tell her children about her history, and her youngest son still doesn't know. Her older daughter, however, discovered her mother's true identity after finding an old bank card.

Mae maintained contact with her mother for a decade after her incarceration. But, when she started demanding her mother tell her the truth about her sister, Heather's death, Rose broke all contact with her and removed her from her prison visitors list. Mae says after the birth of her first son, all of her childhood trauma came rushing back, and she stayed inside her house for eight years, essentially becoming a hermit. The public stigmatized her due to her family history. Declining her from getting a visa to Australia, or rejecting her husband after applying for the police department, for example. Mae believes at least 30 more victims are attributed to either her mother, father or both. She does not think her father stopped killing after he buried his last victim at Cromwell Street. She feels he simply started burying the bodies somewhere else.

(*Murphy, 2018, Buckland, 2018*).

During the trial, it would emerge that the West children were admitted to the local emergency room 31 times between them. Despite this excessive number of injuries, no alarm bells went off in the heads of the medical community workers, nor were social workers ever actively alerted to the goings-on with these children. Anna Marie would reveal horrifying details about the rapes and beatings she endured at the hands of her parents from the age of eight. She said her mother would tell her there was nothing strange about a father having sex with his daughter, and "*everyone did it.*" Anna Marie attempted suicide in 1999 but thankfully survived.

Stephen West, the oldest of the West boys, attempted suicide in 2002 after he was arrested and jailed for raping a 14-year-old girl. He told the court at the time, "*There's a bit of my dad in me.*" This frightening repetition of history can only make one wonder if the legacy of Rose and Fred is set to continue.

Tara West would later tell the media she did not receive the same treatment as her siblings. She believes her mother felt bad for her because Fred was not her father and only gave her light beatings with a wooden spoon. Fred never raped Tara, and she would later say that she believed he was only sexually interested in his biological daughters, and that is why Fred spared her from the sexual abuse.

Barry West would later reveal that at seven years old, he witnessed the murder of his sister, Heather. Stating, he saw his mother jump on Heather's head five times, and then she did not move again.

The sister of one of the Wests' victims, Lucy Partington, who authorities found her decapitated body in the Cromwell Street basement, believes Fred and Rose named their daughter, Lucyanna, after her sister.

(*Kindon, 2019*).

In 2019, the British newspaper *The Mirror* reported that Rose had been involved in several relationships with female inmates while in prison. Rose's previous solicitor revealed the most shocking pairing in a book he wrote about his ex-client. Rose was allegedly involved in a relationship with a fellow convicted female serial killer Myra Hindley. She told Leo Goatley. Myra Hindley, convicted along with her lover, Ian Brady, of four child murders in 1987. When the two women met, quite by chance in jail, Rose said they got along really well and started a relationship. She told Goatley she was impressed by Myra's intelligence taking several university courses while in prison.

Months later, when Goatley revisited Rose, telling him, she called off the relationship with Hindley. Stating Myra was very manipulative and felt that Myra was trying to use her to get things she wanted from the outside and special treatment inside the prison. Rose allegedly referred to Hindley as *"very dangerous."* Hindley died in jail in 2002 at the age of 60.

(*Lo, 2019*)

Although it is hardly unbelievable that these two women would end up in the same prison together at the same time, it is truly frightening how drawn they were to one another. This odd union perhaps speaks to the same attraction that saw Fred and Rose pairing up. From a psychological perspective, it makes sense that anyone would be attracted to someone who displays similar personality traits.

As human beings, we like to be around people who have the same beliefs and values to us as it makes our lives more comfortable. Although we would like to believe that people like Rose would seek out others who are equally disturbed, it may just be as simple as wanting to be around someone who understands you. We all want that, and I don't think Rose found many people in her life that did understand her. Even her children, who spent most of their time with her, struggled to define who their mother was.

Fred and Rosemary West both displayed narcissistic and antisocial personality traits as well as aspects of psychopathy. They both had equally horrendous childhoods, which likely helped develop them into the people they were. Their horrible childhoods, however, cannot be used to excuse their behavior. They both had many siblings who grew up in the same environment they did but didn't end up as serial killers. The most significant component of why Fred and Rose became who they did is choice. They were disturbed and damaged, but instead of taking that out on their victims, they could have sought psychological help. While, as humans, it is only natural for us to have empathy for the children that Fred and Rose once were, this doesn't stop us from expecting them to pay for the horrendous crimes they committed as adults. One does not counter the other.

Separately, they would probably have committed crimes to some extent, but when some sordid twist of fate placed them on the same path, their futures became horrifically entwined with those of their children and their victims. People widely believe the West's killed far more than 12 women, and, to this day, many of their victims lay in graves dug for them, waiting to be discovered and denied justice.

CHAPTER 6

GONE FOR A WALK

On the 20th of September 2014, 37-year-old Tammy Kingery changed out of her work clothes and into her pajamas. Just minutes before, she had been at her job at a care home for the elderly. She was feeling odd all day. Having been diagnosed with mild depression, she didn't think the way she was feeling was related to that. *"Raised blood pressure."* Her coworkers would later say. She tested it four times during the short time she had been at work, and on each time, it indicated high.

Besides the physical feelings, Tammy was not acting like herself either. The usually quiet and professional blond mother and wife earned herself a reputation as her elderly patients' favorite caregiver because she was calm and pleasant. Quite the contrast, that morning, Tammy had been agitated and speaking loudly. Her coworkers tried calming her down, fearing that her behavior was pushing her blood pressure up.

Eventually, although she had driven herself to work that morning, Tammy called her husband to collect her and take her home. As she prepared herself for a nap, her husband decided to take the children out to give her time to rest. Hours later, he would return to an empty house. The door to the bedroom in which Tammy had been sleeping was wide open. Tammy left a note on the kitchen counter, saying she left. It read, "Gone for a walk. Be back soon. Love you."

Tammy Kingery would not be back soon. She would not be back at all. Six years later, her family is still desperately searching for answers, but the deeper they and authorities dig, the more the puzzle seems to deepen, and they find many more questions than answers.

Tammy

Tammy Kingery lived with her husband Park and their three children Caitlyn, Cameron, and Carter. Two of the children were in their teens, and the third was still a toddler when their mother disappeared. In 2001, Tammy completed a nursing degree and then went on to work at a frail care home. Tammy was a highly valued employee at the nursing home, and she hardly ever missed a day of work.

But, when diagnosed with depression in the weeks leading up to her disappearance, she started to take more sick days, which was entirely unlike her. Tammy was extremely committed to her patients at the care home and would become very close to them, even attending their funerals when they passed away and speaking about who they were as people. Her depression also started to affect her home life as she would come home from work and go straight to bed. Some time into her illness, she began to experience insomnia.

Tammy had a very close relationship with her sisters and would speak to them on the phone daily. Her sisters had become extremely concerned about her mental health and the physical effect it was having, encouraging her to see a doctor. Some sources had said in the weeks before her disappearance that she attempted to commit suicide. It is confirmed, though, by her sisters, that several years before her disappearance, Tammy made an unsuccessful attempt at taking her life. She seemed to want to get better, though, as she did make an appointment with her doctor. Sadly, the appointment was for the day after she went missing. Tammy was known as a happy and upbeat person, so her sudden tumble into a bottomless pit of depression concerned her loved ones.

Tammy married her husband Park when she was just 19 years old, and they started having children soon after. They met at a drugstore at which they both worked. By all accounts, Tammy was deeply committed to her family and adored her children.

Gone

When Tammy's husband Park returned after his errands to find Tammy no longer at home, he found it strange that she left a note. According to Park, this was not their usual method of communication, and if Tammy wanted to tell him something, she would usually have sent a text message to his cellphone. Then, he saw something that was even stranger. Tammy left her handbag, cell phone, and keys at home. While it wouldn't be unusual to leave your purse behind if you were just going for a walk, most people would take their cell phones, especially a mother of three children, and the house keys still laying on the counter were the strangest of all.

The house was locked up when Park got there. It was possible to latch the door and pull it shut to lock it as you left, but it made no sense that Tammy would do that, considering she would lock herself out when she got home from her walk. Park would later say knowing his wife's mental state at the time. He immediately became concerned for her safety. He instructed his 13-year-old son to look after his younger brother, and Park headed out in the car to look for Tammy. Thinking perhaps Tammy walked back to work to collect her car, Park drove past the *care home*. Tammy was not there. He then drove around the area for about an hour without success. Park called his oldest daughter Caitlyn, who was sleeping over at a friend's house the previous night and asked her to have her friend drive her around the area to see if she could spot her mom.

The Kingery home, located in a very rural area, would make it difficult to be seen if going for a walk. Several wooded areas surrounded their house. Her family said Tammy has never shown any interest in walking in the woods, as they were quite tricky to navigate. Having searched most of the area, Park returned home, and soon afterward, his daughter Caitlyn also arrived with her friend. The pair told Park they were pretty sure they had just seen Tammy on the back of a motorcycle. Although they couldn't see her face, both Caitlyn and her friend said the long blond hair streaming out from under the helmet and the body type, definitely looked like Tammy. They tried to follow the motorbike, but they were unable to keep up with it. A neighbor would later say they were sure they heard a motorbike engine on the driveway of the Kingery home on the day that Tammy disappeared.

Park started a search with volunteers in the woods around their home and, after finding nothing, at 2 pm, he called police to open a missing person's case. Police examined the crime scene immediately, searching the house looking for any sign indicating forceful entry or foul play. Police found nothing suggesting this. The search was expanded and would eventually include scent dogs (*who could not pick up any scent from Tammy outside of the house*), helicopters, hundreds of police officers, and volunteers.

Tammy's sightings were called in by the public in the days after her disappearance, but none could be confirmed. About a week after Tammy disappeared, Park held another search of the woods, deep into the area, volunteers smelled the scent of decomposition. Nearby, they found a derelict shack inside, a bag with the remains of a deceased dog. Although strange, the discovery didn't seem to be related to Tammy at all. Park reported this discovery to the police. They acknowledged they also found this shack in their searches and decided it did not have any connection to the case.

Initially, police took the decision not to release information about Tammy's depression to the public, as they did not want to create false leads or lead people to make assumptions about why she disappeared. This action is probably the most responsible tack to have taken. It is very likely people hearing this information would have automatically assumed Tammy had gone somewhere to commit suicide, and they would no longer be actively looking out for her. Quite likely, they also didn't want this narrative to get fed back to her children, who, at this point, were still hoping their mother would return home safely.

As part of the investigation, police searched all of Tammy's digital devices for any clues to her whereabouts. On her cellphone, they discovered Tammy had been sending text messages to two men, and the text messages referred to as being *"romantic"* in nature. Police investigated both men thoroughly, and according to police, were found to have nothing to do with Tammy's disappearance. These messages, though, sparked questions about the state of the Kingerys' marriage.

Park admitted their relationship was strained and had been for many years since Tammy was unfaithful once before. Park said Tammy asked him for a divorce, but he refused, saying he wanted to work on their marriage. Park felt that Tammy only ever spoke about divorce when she was deeply depressed, and when she would come out of her depression, she made no mention of it. Park said he wanted to stick by Tammy and help her to work through her depression, which is why he refused a divorce. Police also investigated Park Kingery but found no evidence involving him in Tammy's disappearance.

The note allegedly left behind by Tammy was also looked at to ensure that she wrote it. There was, of course, a possibility that someone, having taken Tammy, wrote the note to throw her husband and police off track. After all, Park said it was odd for Tammy to have written a note. Police did eventually confirm the handwriting analysis and fingerprinting proved Tammy did, indeed, write the letter.

(*Where is Tammy Kingery, 2018*).

More Missing Women

Tammy's case would remain quiet for two years. Park Kingery, unable to cope with one salary financially, was forced to sell the couple's home and declare bankruptcy. He moved in with his parents. Nothing was ever heard from Tammy again, and the leads and sightings began to dry up. Park withdrew the reward money he offered for information on Tammy's whereabouts when he fell into financial difficulties.

Almost two years after Tammy Kingery disappeared, another woman went missing not far from the area Tammy was last sighted. Kala Brown's case was slightly different. She vanished along with her boyfriend, Charlie Carver. Just two months later, 49-year-old Tracey Wright, seen driving her vehicle (*also close to the two other disappearances*) on the 27th of October 2016, then both she and her car vanished without a trace. Three weeks after Tracey Wright disappeared, police made a discovery that could link all three of these cases together.

In November 2016, Spartanburg County police were at a property investigating a sex crime when they heard banging coming from a metal shipping container. On opening the shipping container, they found Kala Brown, severely dehydrated and restrained with chains. She reported that the owner of the property, Todd Kohlhepp, kidnapped her and her boyfriend, Charlie Carver, in August of that year. She witnessed Kohlhepp shoot her boyfriend to death, and he kept her prisoner ever since. Police found Charlie Carver's body on the grounds buried in a shallow grave and arrested Kohlhepp later that day. After his arrest, he pointed out another two gravesites on his property and told the police he was responsible for four murders in 2003 at a bike shop, where four staff members were gunned down. As details of Kohlhepp's modus operandi and area of operation began leaking to the public, the missing person's advocacy agency Missing Pieces Network soon started to question whether Kohlhepp could have been responsible for the disappearances of Tammy Kingery and Tracey Wright as well.

(*NBC News, 2016*).

The two bodies on Todd's property were not Tammy and Tracey. They belonged to a couple named Megan and Johnny Coxie, who went missing in 2015. As Kohlhepp went to trial, his true nature and the psychological profiling done on him revealed that he possibly had more than the seven victims that police knew about.

Who Is Todd Kohlhepp?

At the time of his arrest, Todd Kohlhepp was 45 years old. He worked as a successful real estate agent and was well-liked. Kohlhepp is intelligent with an IQ that tested 118. Criminal profiler John Douglas found Todd to be helpful in his analysis of himself. Stating that the man, now convicted of seven murders and technically a serial killer, was so intrigued by the peculiarities of his psyche, adding additional pages to Douglas' standard question-naire, giving him more information. Todd was born on the 7th of March 1971 in Florida, and his parents divorced when he was a toddler. At first, he lived with his mother and stepfather in South Carolina, but at the age of 12, he moved to Arizona to live with his father.

While living in Arizona at age 15, he committed his first sexually motivated crime. Todd kidnapped a 14-year-old girl at gunpoint, held her hostage, and raped her. He then threatened to kill her family before releasing her. The terrified young woman did go to the police, and the police charged Todd with kidnapping and assault. In the trial and investigation, for that case, an array of skeletons fell out of the Kohlhepp family closet. Todd experienced an extremely violent childhood in a dysfunctional family and exhibited violent behaviors from an early age. Todd, at the age of nine, was admitted for psychiatric observation, for the first time. The judge sentenced Todd to 15 years in an adult jail for his crimes. He served 14 years and released in 2001. Todd had to register as a sex offender and decided to move back to South Carolina. He earned two bachelor's degrees and then started working as a real estate agent.

During his interview with John Douglas, he claimed there were two more victims police didn't know. Todd didn't name the victims or provide locations for their bodies, but John Douglas says that he was so specific about the details of the crimes that he tends to believe the stories were true.

(*Finn, 2019*).

This event wasn't the only time Todd had spoken about other victims. He also told Kala Brown, while he held her captive, that his victims were "in the high double-digits." He said the same thing to a reporter who interviewed him. In this interview, he bragged about his private pilot's license, which he earned in 2006, helped him in hiding bodies so well the police would never find them. Todd Kohlhepp was not necessarily motivated by sexual deviancy, despite some of his crimes having a sexual element. He seemed to kill often out of retaliation for a perceived wrong. Todd had connections to all of his victims. He has been a customer of the bike shop at which he murdered four employees. Kala Brown and her boyfriend had been at his property to do work for him. He was known to the Coxie couple as well. All of these connections were so remote the police would never have knocked on his door in an investigation, but those connections were just close enough to pique a killer's interest.

(*The Murder Squad, 2019*)

What Happened to Tammy Kingery?

Tammy Kingery has now been missing for six years. Her two older children are now adults. The youngest, who was just a toddler when his mother disappeared, likely has very few memories of the mother he lost. There are several theories about what could have happened to Tammy.

Suicide

Tammy attempted suicide in the past and struggled with depression in the weeks before her disappearance. She was on medication, but this is not a safeguard from depression deepening to the extent that she may have wanted to harm herself. Many will say she would never have left her children, and she loved them too much to commit suicide. Mental illness doesn't work that way. Unfortunately, love cannot heal depression, and, often, the sufferer believes they are doing a good thing for their family by committing suicide as they feel like a burden. The nature of depression means that no matter how often someone tells you that you are not a burden, it is difficult to believe. This downward spiral in Tammy's mental health indeed points to the possibility that she left the house that day to take her life.

On the day of her disappearance, she behaved strangely and in a manner that was not necessarily congruent with depression. Tammy's manic behavior that morning points more toward bipolar disorder in which the sufferer cycles between depression and mania. People with bipolar disorder are also known to undertake risk-taking behavior, and this could explain Tammy's infidelity, with her interactions with several men at once, at least on her phone. If Tammy had bipolar disorder, it is possible, after that manic episode, she cycled into a deep depression and decided to take her life. This theory would explain why she left all of her belongings at home and locked the door behind her.

There was no proof, however, that Tammy had taken any means to take her life. People who are suicidal are also not usually concerned with anyone finding their body. Many people will commit suicide in their homes in the full knowledge that their families will find them. This action is not done maliciously, of course, but is simply part of the skewed thinking process of the suicidal person. That is why, even if Tammy decided to go into the woods and commit suicide, it is far more likely she would have done so in the first secluded area she found. The other thing that makes us wonder whether Tammy committed suicide was the sighting her daughter made of the blond woman on a motorcycle.

New Life

The second theory around Tammy's disappearance is that she left with a man she was having an affair with and started a new life. In today's world, it is difficult, if not impossible, to stay completely off the radar unless you have someone supporting you financially. Tammy's family said she was a very loving person and also a good mother. Would she have left her children wondering, possibly for the rest of their lives, what happened to their mother? She had to have known the impact her disappearance would have from a financial perspective on her children. They lost their home, and their father struggled to support them. Even with mental illness, would she have been able to watch them suffer like that?

The risk-taking side of bipolar disorder (*if indeed that is what Tammy was experiencing*), could have driven her, in a manic state, to believe that leaving and starting a new life was the best thing to do. She wouldn't remain in that state forever, and, if left untreated, her mental health would have continued to deteriorate. She would very likely have come into contact with authorities at some point. This theory seems very unlikely.

Foul Play

Within the foul play theory lays two options:

1. Tammy was taken by a person known/unknown to her from her house by force.

2. She left the house by her own free will, and something went wrong after that.

Police found no evidence of forced entry or a struggle in the Kingery home. The scent dogs could not pick up Tammy's scent outside of the house, which indicates she did not leave on foot, and if she were taken by someone from her home and forced to write the note, handwriting specialists would have picked up some form of variation in her writing style. Imagine if someone is holding a weapon at you while you are writing a note. Chances are there would be displayed variation in your writing. But, there was no indication of this in the letter.

If Tammy left the home of her own free will, perhaps with someone she knew, it would be possible she left her phone and keys there, but why would she leave her handbag? Maybe she hadn't intended to be very long? We know that Tammy was communicating with men on her phone. The two men who police found messages from were investigated and determined not to know her whereabouts. A third man no one knew about could also be possible. Neighbors reported hearing a loud engine in Tammy's driveway that morning. Her daughter and her friend believe they saw her driving off on the back of a motorcycle by a man. So, perhaps Tammy's boyfriend had a bike, and, in her mania, she arranged for him to pick her up and go for a drive. What happened to her after that, though? Tammy may have chosen to get involved with the wrong man, and we have to consider the possibility that the man could be Todd Kohlhepp.

Todd's property was within an hour's drive of Tammy's home. He was a real estate agent and likely worked all over both Spartanburg and McCormick counties. Todd was an attractive man, and he was 42 years old when Tammy disappeared so that she could have seen him as a potential partner. Todd was a customer at the motorcycle shop at which he committed four murders in 2003. Customers of motorcycle shops are very likely to own motorcycles. Todd Kohlhepp had a bike in 2003, but did he own one in 2014, and was he the man Tammy's daughter saw that day? I am confident that authorities would easily be able to confirm or deny this. But, for our purposes, aerial shots of Kohlhepp's property after Kala Brown were found to show two items that look very much like motorcycles.

Is it possible that Todd picked up Tammy that day on his motorcycle (*which would be faster and less identifiable than his truck*) at her request? Perhaps she just wanted to go for a ride and clear her head. It's also possible that in her manic state, Tammy told him she wanted to start a life with him. Did he take her back to his property, and possibly Tammy then changed her mind realizing she had to go home. We know Todd's crimes were retribution based. Did he kill Tammy because she told him she didn't want to stay with him anymore, and she wanted to go home to her children? If he did kill her, maybe he realized there was a rather extensive search conducted by the police for her, and it would be better if Todd used that private plane and pilot's license he bragged about to dispose of her body somewhere else. This theory is all just supposition, of course, and there is absolutely no proof that Todd Kohlhepp had anything to do with Tammy Kingery's disappearance. But it certainly is an interesting possibility.

We must accept that we may never know what happened to Tammy Kingery. But, cold cases are solved every day, and this recent case is undoubtedly not too old to be solved. Although the mystery is profound and the possibilities are almost endless, for the sake of Tammy's three children, we must maintain hope that we will know the truth one day.

CHAPTER 7

GONE GIRL

Listen, can you make sure she stays there. She doesn't know the area, and I don't want to wake up with news she disappeared or dead okay. These words would have significant meaning on the 16th of September 2009, for 24-year-old Mitrice Lavon Richardson.

Mitrice was undoubtedly not herself that day. The young woman was not making sense when she spoke to others. Her garbled, nonsensical statements seemed to indicate that she was experiencing a mental health crisis. After a 40-minute drive to Malibu, the tall, beautiful, dark-haired fashion model and beauty queen would be arrested and briefly held by the police. When officers spoke to her mother on the phone, they assured her they would keep Mitrice safe for the night and could collect her in the morning. They didn't keep that promise. Instead, at close to 1 a.m., claiming that they no longer had reason to hold the young woman, they released her into the darkness of the night, in an area she didn't know, with no car, cell phone, or purse. Mitrice Richardson was never seen again.

A Downhill Slide

Mitrice Richardson was born of an unexpected pregnancy to her mother Latice on the 30th of April 1985. Both Latice and Mitrice's father, Michael, were high school students at the time of Mitrice's birth. Thankfully, Latice was given support by her grandmother, Mildred, and was determined to continue with her schooling and do well to ensure her daughter a successful future. After they graduated, Latice and Michael began working to build a life for their daughter while Mildred cared for Mitrice. However, Michael struggled to justify the hard work he put into his job at a restaurant with a small amount of money he earned from it, and his frustration led him to deal drugs. He started with small amounts, only wanting to supplement his income, but as he realized how easy it was to make money this way, he got more and more involved. Eventually, in 1989, he was arrested, served a prison sentence for his drug crimes, and then released him in 1993.

Latice became involved in another relationship while Michael was in jail and married Larry Sutton, who became Mitrice's stepfather. At this same time, a phenomenon was becoming apparent in the Los Angeles area, which would touch the lives of the Richardson family decades later. Racial tensions built up between the LAPD and the African American community after the brutal beating of Rodney King by several police officers. This case would eventually lead to the Los Angeles riots, which killed 63 people. It was this violence and the growing tensions in the area that prompted Latice and Larry to move their family to the San Gabriel Valley region of Southern California in the hopes of a quieter and safer life. This move would also allow Mitrice to grow up in an area that was not always under threat, and, as such, she blossomed.

Mitrice was highly intelligent and focused. Her mother told her she could be whatever she wanted to be, but Mitrice had to be willing to put in the work and, for the most part, Mitrice listened and poured her heart into anything she did. She was still just a child, though, and as she became a teenager, she did have her moments of being led down the wrong path by friends. Latice made her daughter take responsibility for her actions, though, and as a result, she always found her way back to the straight and narrow. Mitrice was exceptionally athletic and worked hard to develop all of her talents. She was a talented cheerleader and dancer and was said to have an undeniable charisma on stage.

Another aspect of Mitrice's character, which would later become glaringly tragic, was her preference for remaining indoors. Mitrice did not enjoy spending time in nature and would always choose to do crosswords or to write in her journal over any outdoor activity. She also hated having to walk anywhere, and getting her driver's license was a special day for her because it meant she would never have to walk anywhere again, all this time spent inside led to a deep interest in psychology. Mitrice wanted to understand how the human mind worked and what made people do what they did. A development in Mitrice's own life may have also led to her deepening interest in the human mind as, when she was in her first year at college, revealing to her family that she was a lesbian. Thankfully, her family displayed unconditional love, and if Mitrice had been concerned about their rejection based on her sexuality, she had nothing to worry about.

The college that Mitrice chose was a 45-minute drive from her home, so rather than struggle in California traffic every day, she moved in with her great-grand-mother, who lived closer to campus. Mitrice enjoyed college life. She did well academically and got a part-time job at a shipping company where she met her first serious girlfriend, Tessa Moon. She became close with the psychology professors on campus, and as her graduation neared, she planned to attend graduate school. Mitrice took a job dancing at a popular nightclub. It wasn't stripping or exotic dancing, but her family was unhappy with the choice, feeling that it could put her in contact with the wrong people. Mitrice used a stage name, 'Hazel,' and even had business cards printed for herself with her picture and the stage name on them.

Soon after this, Mitrice broke up with Tessa and became obsessed with a woman called Vanessa. The woman was already in a relationship, though, and Mitrice's attention became unwanted. This rejection seemed to spark her downward spiral. Friends would later say that, at this point, Mitrice began to withdraw from them, and she spent most of her time alone and on social media. Her social media posts were constant and becoming increasingly strange and cryptic. Latice realized how badly her daughter's mental health was spiraling when she received a text message from Matrice that was entirely off-topic and made no sense.

(*Trace Evidence Podcast, 2019*).

The Ocean

On the day of her disappearance, Mitrice went to work at the shipping company, left for lunch and never returned. She would usually have dinner with her great-grandmother, but, on this day, she decided that she wanted to drive to see the ocean instead. Mildred would later say that Mitrice seemed fine when she left, at about 5 p.m., for the 40-minute drive to Malibu. It appears that Mitrice did not drive directly to Malibu, though, as at some time between 5 p.m. and 7 p.m. that night, her aunt arrived at her home to find Mitrice's business cards scattered all over the lawn and on the stairs.

Her aunt also found a cryptic note underneath the window wiper of her husband's vehicle. It read "Black woman scorned," and she had drawn a smiley face next to the words. The meaning of this note is unknown to this day. Did Mitrice want to knock on her aunt's door for help, but instead started digging around in her bag for something to write a note on, accidentally spilled her business cards on the steps? Why hadn't she picked them up? Or was this her way of making a statement about her family's disapproval of her dancing job? Mitrice's aunt, although thinking the situation was strange, did not try to contact her niece at that time.

Mitrice believed to have arrived in Malibu around 7 p.m. that night. She would have had enough time to watch the sunset on the beach before getting back into her '98 Honda Civic and continuing along the highway until she reached a restaurant called Geoffrey's. The restaurant, reserved for Malibu locals and travelers with deep pockets, was upmarket and high-priced. This fact would have been evident to Mitrice when she pulled into the parking lot and found valet parking cars. The valet was in the process of parking another person's car and told Mitrice he would be with her in a moment. When he returned, the valet found that Mitrice got out of her vehicle and into his car. She was rifling through his CDs. The valet asked her what she was doing, and her response was nonsensical. He didn't feel that she was drunk as her movements were fluid, and she was not stumbling or slurring, but what was coming out of her mouth did not make any sense. Mitrice then gave the valet her keys and asked him if Vanessa was inside. This mention of Vanessa, who she developed an obsession over, seems to be a clear indication that Mitrice was losing touch with reality. Vanessa would later confirm to police that she'd never been to the restaurant, nor made any plans to meet Mitrice there that night, and this was confirmed. Mitrice entered the restaurant, and the valet followed her, warning the front of the house staff to watch the woman as she was behaving strangely.

Mitrice took a table on her own and ordered a cock-tail and a steak dinner. When her cocktail arrived, she picked it up and walked over to another table occupied by a party of seven. Without requesting permission, she joined the table and drank her cocktail. Besides her odd behavior, Mitrice didn't fit in with the restaurant's other customers. Her outfit—a Bob Marley t-shirt with a long-sleeved shirt underneath. Van shoes, pink alligator belt, and Rastafarian hat—stood out, and the customers at the table said she made little sense when speaking to them, talking about astrology and other esoteric subjects. When her meal arrived, Matrice went back to her table, ate alone, and joined the group again. When the table got up to leave, Mitrice stood up with them and tried to go.

The restaurant manager stopped her and reminded her that she hadn't paid her bill yet. The young woman protested that the party of seven had paid her bill but eventually relented and told the manager that she was from Mars and had no money to pay the bill. The restaurant called the police, and while they were en route, the hostess called Mitrice's great-grandmother on her request. Mildred offered to pay the bill by providing her credit card details over the phone, but the hostess said they were only allowed to make payments in person. When three deputies arrived, they spoke with Mildred on the phone, and so did Mitrice. Mildred would later say that her great-granddaughter was not in her right mind and didn't seem to comprehend that the police were arresting her. The deputies took Mitrice outside to her vehicle, which they searched.

Allegedly, the car was filthy, filled with papers and debris. While they could not find her wallet, they did obtain her driver's license, a small amount of marijuana, and an almost empty bottle of alcohol. The restaurant staff considered banding together to pay Mitrice's bill to avoid her arrest. But, they eventually decided it would probably be better for her if she were not allowed to drive off on her own as her behavior was so erratic. Mitrice passed a field sobriety test, indicating that some form of intoxication did not cause her reaction. The restaurant owner stated that he wished to press charges against Mitrice, so she was handcuffed and taken to the Lost Hills Sheriff's Station. Her vehicle was towed and impounded.

On hearing about her daughter's situation from Mildred, Latice phoned the Lost Hills Sheriff's Office and spoke to one of the deputies. Latice specifically asked if Mitrice would be released that night, and they told her she would not be, and she could collect her daughter in the morning.

In a sad twist of fate, Latice jokingly reported saying to the deputy something along the lines of, "her daughter didn't know the area, and didn't want to wake up to the news that her daughter had disappeared or murdered."

When the deputy put together the report of Mitrice's arrest, no mention was made of her odd behavior that night. She was charged with possession of marijuana and defrauding an innkeeper. Had the deputy acknowledged the signs that Mitrice was in mental distress, they were required legally to hold her for longer or even put her into a 72-hour mental health hold. During which they would evaluate her mental condition. Unfortunately, they did not provide any assistance. Mitrice made four phone calls from the police station that night, but none of them were to her mother or great-grandmother. The line on which she made these calls were not recorded.

(*Trace Evidence Podcast, 2019*).

Gone

The next day, Latice decided to let her daughter stew a little to learn her lesson, and at around 5 a.m., she called the Sheriff's office to inquire about how much money she would need to bail her daughter out. The deputies told her that Mitrice was no longer in custody and released her early that morning. The police would later claim they released Mitrice because the charges were not severe enough to hold her overnight. They would also argue they offered to let Mitrice stay in a cell or the lobby until morning, but she refused. When released, she had her driver's license and the keys to her vehicle, that the police impounded in a yard 15 miles away. No one offered her a ride to a safe place.

Latice called the Sheriff's department back 15 minutes later and asked if she could file a missing person's report for Mitrice. But, the Sheriff recommended she wait 24 hours unless there were extenuating circumstances. Latice agreed to wait a few more hours in case Mitrice turned up.

On the morning after Mitrice's release, a resident called in to report that a young woman walked through his property, and he had seen her sitting outside his window. He asked her if she needed help, but the woman told him she was resting. When he went back a few minutes later, she was gone. The woman matched Mitrice's description. The resident's property was rural and about six miles from the police station. A deputy responded but could find no trace of the woman. When Latice arrived at the Sheriff's department, they told her about the call, and she headed out to the area. On seeing how rural it was, she immediately believed her daughter must have been given a ride to the area as there was no way she would have walked that far on her own. Despite Mitrice's dislike for the outdoors and hiking, also considering that if she was indeed experiencing a mental breakdown, her behavior couldn't be from a rational perspective.

The first official search for Mitrice commenced 48 hours after her disappearance due to jurisdictional confusion. A scent-tracking dog was brought in and was unable to pick up any trace outside of the police station. Police then took the dogs to the man's home, who claimed to have seen a woman in his yard. The dogs did pick up Mitrice's scent, indicating that it was her sitting outside. The dog then led investigators to another nearby residence where the trail ended. Police found footprints nearby, which matched the tread of the Van shoes that Mitrice was wearing. Trackers were able to determine that she intermittently walked, picked up speed, and broken into a full run, only to slow down and walk again.

In the days following Mitrice's disappearance, her case was moved between departments. Although there was allegedly no evidence supporting murder, police handed the case over to a murder and robbery investigation team. These new investigators started by searching Mitrice's car, which, strangely, no one had done yet. They found her wallet and cell phone inside. Inside her purse was her bank card, and her account had over $ 2,000 in it. This evidence was significant because she could have just paid her restaurant bill that night. Perhaps, a further indication that Mitrice was experiencing a severe mental break down, to the point of not knowing she could pay her bill. As far as the field sobriety test indicated, she was not drunk or on drugs, so what else, besides a signif-icant mental illness. What could have caused this strange behavior? Perhaps, deep down, in some untainted part of her consciousness, she knew that she needed help, and getting arrested seemed the only way to achieve that, at the time. Forensic psychologists would review Mitrice's journals as part of the investigation and determined that there was a good possibility that she had bipolar disorder.

(*Trace Evidence Podcast, 2019*).

Police Inaction

As the weeks ticked by with no sign of Mitrice, the public, press, and her family soon turned against the police. Allegedly, they had not treated Mitrice the way that they would have treated a young white woman. The family demanded to see the CCTV footage from the cells taken the night that Mitrice had been there, and while the police initially claimed that the cameras did not record, this was later proven not to be true. An email came up, stating the deputy felt uneasy about releasing her due to her distressed mental state. Proof that statements were inconsistent. Later, the deputy claimed to have no memory of typing this email. Mitrice's family hired a civil rights lawyer and got a local councilwoman on board to address how the police violated her civil rights as a disabled person (*referring to her apparent mental illness*), which led to her disappearance. The family worked the area hard over the next few months, handing out flyers and searching to no avail.

In January 2009, the city launched its most extensive search, in 20 years of Los Angeles history, in the area surrounding where the dogs last confirmed Mitrice's scent. The dogs did not find a single piece of evidence. In March of that year, Mitrice's father, Michael, claimed to have seen his daughter in Las Vegas working as a prostitute. He said that he had called her name, but she ran off into a crowd and lost her. When the family was eventually allowed to view the footage of the police body cams from that night, you can see a deputy exiting the building directly after Mitrice. Despite being told, no deputies were available when Mitrice was released. This deputy would be questioned and claimed that he did not have any interaction with Mitrice that night.

By 2010, Mitrice had been missing for almost two years, with still no sign of her. There were a few more sightings of a woman matching Mitrice's description in Las Vegas, but none of these leads ever went anywhere. Eventually, the investigation team called off the case. The case was going cold.

(*Trace Evidence Podcast, 2019*).

Discovery

On the 9th of August 2009, two park rangers were hiking in a canyon, which was very difficult to get into, approximately two miles from where the man reported last seeing Mitrice. The canyon had been the scene of a busted marijuana farm months before, and rangers wanted to check that no new activity had started. As they descended into the canyon, they discovered a skull with black hair still attached. The police identified the remains as Mitrice Richardson. Several inconsistencies and poor practices would plague the investigation. The removal of Mitrice's remains had unexplained delays in getting to the coroner. The remains being moved by police despite them being told not to do so. Investigators would find the rest of Mitrice's remains approximately six feet from her skull.

(*Kessler, 2011*)

Despite the strange positioning of some limbs and other parts of her remains, there were no signs of animal activity around the body. There was also no sign of trauma to her body, so the corner could not determine the manner been of death as a homicide. What struck her family, Mitrice's body was completely nude. There was no damage to her clothes, in Malibu's searing temperatures, or signs of the clothes tearing off her body. A private pathologist would later state that the clothes did not look exposed to the elements for 11 months. She was undressed, Her clothing scattered throughout the canyon, whether by herself or someone else.

The remains themselves also presented questions. For instance, if Mitrice's body had indeed laid in the canyon for that amount of time, in Malibu's searing temperatures, it should have been entirely skeletonized. But, it wasn't, she seemed to be partially mummified, much soft tissue remained. Despite all of these inconsistencies, police continued to insist there was no reason to deem the death a homicide. Therefore, they didn't treat the location as a crime scene, nor did it separate her clothing for testing, nor was the area around her body protected for forensic analysis. In 2011 Mitrice's body was exhumed at her family's request, but, again, the police pathologist found that there was no way to determine her cause of death, and there were no signs of homicide.

(*Trace Evidence Podcast, 2019*).

Several months after the discovery, the poor quality of investigation done at the site would be brought to the forefront when Mitrice's friends and family hiked to the area where they found her body to set up a memorial. As they dug in the dirt and erected plastic flowers, they uncovered Mitrice's finger bones. In the years that followed, Latice and Michael both successfully sued the police department for failing to protect Mitrice that night, although they would never admit to any wrongdoing.

(*Kessler, 2011*)

The Unknown

Mitrice Richardson was on her way to graduate school and have a successful life. She was young and beautiful, but due to possibly undiagnosed mental illness, she was also vulnerable. Many small changes could have been made on the night of Mitrice's disappearance, giving a different outcome to this case, and whether the police department held a duty of care to her, is still undetermined. The fact that Mitrice was experiencing some sort of mental breakdown is evident. What is not clear, however, is what happened to her after she left the police station. The fact that the scent dog picked up no trace of her directly outside the police station indicates that she may have gotten into a vehicle. Indeed, it seems unlikely that she would have walked six miles to the resident's home. Why does her scent stop at the second house, and what was she running from?

Her body and clothes did not appear to have been in that canyon for 11 months, but only a private pathologist would acknowledge that. So where was her body during that time, if she was not there? Did Mitrice die on the night she disappeared, whether at the hands of someone else or by accident, or was she kept somewhere for a time and then killed and dumped?

Sadly, friends and family have had to come to terms with the fact that they will, possibly, never know the truth. Mitrice Richardson lost her life under the most bizarre circumstances, and if someone is responsible for her death, they have never revealed their secret.

CHAPTER 8

STORIES OF A CARTEL ASSASSIN

"We had no plans to start killing people,
but it did turn out that way."
-Jorge Ayala-Rivera

There is a stereotypical image of a hitman, the kind that dots thrillers like the Hitman franchise and John Wick. In popular culture, these are cold, efficient, broody, concise, and stoic masterminds with a high degree of discipline. Jorge "Rivi" Ayala was a different sort of hitman. He traded the coldness for a little faux compassion. Sometimes actual pain bought the stoicism and asceticism for overindulgence. He was ruthless but not always efficient and lucky, breaking the perceived flawless efficiency that dots the lives of his fictional counterparts. However, he has a silver tongue that Jimmy Mcgill would envy.

Jorge Ayala Rivi's tale is easily the stuff of urban legends, with twists and turns and enough sex, drugs, and violence to keep you interested. You don't often hear podcasters talk about confessed unapologetic killers with a tone that teeters closer to admiration. This story is a testament to the man's infectious nature and how his tale unfolds from relatively dull beginnings to a contract killer.

The start of a new career

Jorge Ayala Rivi was born in Cali, Columbia. When he was young, his father escaped life in Columbia. A life that was often fraught with violence and marauding gangs. He moved to Chicago, where he worked at General Motors. Rivi became a mechanic for his father. It was while working for his father that Rivi learned how to break into cars. This deviant behavior escalated into stealing cars and selling them to chop shops. He quickly put a team together that would help him take more cars and make more money. He and his group became the most prominent car thieves in Chicago. It would be this activity that would lead to a series of unlikely, chance events that ultimately defined his life.

Rivi didn't have a hard life. He lived comfortably. Rivi started down this road out of an unexplainable passion for criminal life. Perhaps he had a personality that made him especially drawn towards this type of life, or maybe he never really felt like the average life wasn't exciting enough.

It makes you wonder about the nature of life; how doing something straightforward can inadvertently lead to consequences that seem almost unthinkable. If there is one thing that Rivi's story illustrates, it's this quicksand nature of life. A slippery slope analogy to what happened to him wouldn't be an accurate characterization, because the journey isn't one of steep dive into the underbelly of crime. It is a story dotted with luck, sharp turns and blunders, and unforeseen consequences. You know, like real life? The sheer messiness and unpredictableness of it make for a story that shows how limited the control we can exert on our lives truly is.

For Rivi, it all started one day when he stole the wrong car or the right vehicle, depending on how you see things. The following day, cartel members found him. They asked if he took their car. According to Rivi, he told them he had the car and that they needed to give him 500 dollars, then he would give it back. Instead of threatening Rivi, they were impressed by his courage, so they gave him a job. They showed him some guns they'd hidden in the trunk, and they asked him to deliver them to Miami.

Investigators aren't to convinced this is what happened. It seemed likely the Cartel members told Rivi to take the guns to Miami or face grave consequences. This assignment was risky. Investigators claim it wasn't an act showing how impressed they were of Rivi, or how much they respected him, regardless, Rivi and his associates drove the guns down to Miami. When he got to Miami, he stayed for a while. He started doing odd jobs for the cartel, low-level crimes like doing collections. He was getting paid $1000 a day. "That was the first time we were working with people that were in the drug business. We had no plans to start killing people, but it turned out that way."

(*Corben, 2006*).

A couple of weeks later, Rivi and some of his friends found themselves at a Columbian nightclub. One of their drug carriers told them to get out because there would be a hit in the club. They were going for the table right next to them. He thanked him for the warning and asked to get his friends before he leaves. He inadvertently sabotaged the hit when he told one of his associates that they should leave because there was going to be a shooting. His associate informed the men who were targets. This mistake happened because Rivi didn't tell him who the targets were. "It was an accident. My friend knew one of the guys at the table. He was just looking after his friends," Rivi said.

Rivi was summoned and taken by the hitman to there boss, where he would answer for what he'd done. He escaped a worse fate by being allowed to fix what he had done. As a way to redeem himself, Rivi had to find the target and kill them. Rivi agreed, seeing there was no other way out of the situation.

Cartel Queen

The boss, who had ordered the hit was Griselda Blanco, the godmother. She was one of the most significant cocaine traffickers in the city, controlling about 70 percent of the market, and she was known for being extraordinarily bloodthirsty. It is hard to speak of Rivi's story because she was the one calling the shots, much of what happened to Rivi because of her business. Griselda is a planet on her own, and Rivi, though a titan in his own right, was caught in its orbit, unable to shake his loyalty. Griselda was brutal. She overlooked the common courtesy that gangs gave to each other in times of war; she often killed quickly and easily. "She was the biggest back then. Griselda was the godmother of cocaine," Rivi would say about her, with a face wrought with a strange mixture of admiration and amazement.

(*Corben, 2006*).

In times of war, people try to avoid casualties if they can. They sometimes leave the kids out of it. They don't shoot each other at funerals, and they sure as hell don't at weddings. But Griselda couldn't be stopped. Regarding the botched attempt, Griselda told Rivi she was only interested in two brothers at the table, yet she prepared to take anyone at the table if it meant they would be dead too.

Griselda: "I am only interested in the two brothers, the other four were gonna get hit because they were sitting at the table."

Rivi: "You were going to kill four people just to get the two?"

Griselda: "That is how I do my things. Spray the whole,"

Rivi spoke about the event, expressing his shock as she spoke about the unorthodox methods. "That surprised me." If she wanted someone dead, she wanted it, no matter who was in their way, and if you can make it hurt, do it. Griselda thought to have ordered the killings of more than 200 people. In her position, she struck terror in many. Rivi would become her biggest enforcer, collecting on loans, completing hits, and doing whatever else she asked of him. "Griselda was calling the shots. Whatever she said everybody stayed quiet, nobody gave an opinion," Rivi would say years later, reflecting on the events.

(*Corben, 2006*)

Rivi was offered 50,000 dollars for each brother if he completed the task. This job, regardless of how it looked, would prove to be an excellent opportunity for him.

Rivi had a week to deliver on his promise. One of his associates at the hotel told him he could get one of the guys who belonged to the group. Then they would use him to find others. They set up a meeting and kidnapped him. "We beat him, no answer. The second day we beat him, no answer. The third day I was losing hope. Four days we beat, we get an answer."

(*Corben, 2006*)

Their prisoner set up a meeting for them with one of the brothers at the Ramada Inn. Rivi and his associates went there, got the brother, and delivered him to Griselda. Over dinner the next day, Griselda would tell Rivi what she did to the man. Griselda shot him, and her man cut him up into pieces, packed him in a box, wrapped a bow around it, and left it at the turnpike. Rivi was visibly shocked by how she told the story with such ease as if it was a typical day in her life. "She said she likes cutting people up."

(Corben, 2006)

His next job would come when one of Griselda's former associates betrayed her. His name was Oscar Piedrahita. He was in charge of smuggling cocaine for Griselda into the United States from Columbia. As time went on, he kidnapped Griselda's son and demanded a ransom of 5 million dollars. Griselda gave him the money, got her son back, and then Oscar disappeared. But she never forgot.

When Rivi started working for her, Griselda mentioned Oscar to him. She told him she wants him dead if he ever finds him. On one auspicious day, as Rivi was reading The Miami Herald, he saw a story in the obituary section about a drowned kid. The father was Oscar Piedrahita, and an address was listed. Rivi told Griselda about it. He asked for someone who can escort him to the wake and point Oscar out to him. Griselda and Griselda's men, including Rivi, went to the wake. They lured Oscar out by asking for him outside. And when he stepped out into the driveway, he was shot with a machine gun. He died right there in the driveway. The story made headlines. "It's sad that he had to die at his son's wake. But he chose that when he messed with this lady. Business is business," Rivi said.

(*Corben, 2006*)

A hefty price to pay

One night, Griselda's son drove on the front lawn of Chucho, one of Griselda's associates, he wanted to spend the night there with his girlfriend as he was coming from the club nearby. Chucho got into an argument with Griselda's son. Griselda's son tried using his mother's name to get what he wanted. Cucho said, "I Don't give a fuck who you tell. I don't give a fuck about your mom, tell your mother I said to fuck herself. Get back in your car, get out of here. Tell your mother I kicked your ass…" Chucho kicked him in the ass said Rivi as he recounted

Cucho's story. "That was one thing about her. You could never touch her kids."

The next day, she told Rivi that she wanted Chucho dead. That the next time Rivi sees him, he should kill him. As usual, she put a price on his head. Rivi and his associates did not hesitate. "It was not going to be easy because he is good. One mistake wasn't gonna get him, or we were gonna get killed," Rivi said in an interview.

(Corben, 2006)

Rivi and his associates got in a white van. They were equipping themselves with M16 rifles. Chucho was driving down US 1 when he and his associates started driving parallel to Chucho. Once they got clear, they fired at Chucho's car. They hit the tires, and Chucho lost control before regaining it and escaping. They got a call later from Griselda, saying Chucho's son was in the backseat of the car and got shot in the scuffle. He was dead—a hefty price to pay for a small altercation. Rivi said that if he had known, he would have never shot at the car.

Regardless, Chucho was angry and threatened to kill Rivi. There was a warrant for Chucho's arrest from the DEA at the time, so he didn't report what happened to the police. He took his son's body, put it in the bathtub, and filled it with ice to preserve the body overnight. The following day, he called the police anonymously so they could find his body. The child was wrapped in sheets, left at a mosque with three roses and a passport. He was just about to turn three years old.

Hitman's code

Griselda gave five kilos of cocaine to Alfredo Lorenzo on consignment, giving him two weeks to pay the debt. The two weeks passed with no payment, so Rivi was sent to collect the debt. Alfredo gave him the runaround. He reported this to Griselda, who told Rivi to kill him. Rivi returned with two of his associates. They knocked on the door, Alfredo answered, and they put a gun in his face, telling him to be quiet. They asked him where his wife was. She was in the kitchen, and so they got her. Alfredo had three kids, two girls, one six the other four years old, and a boy who was just a baby.

The plan was only to kill Alfredo, so Oscar, one of the other assassins with Rivi, took him to the bedroom and shot him two times in the head. Rivi heard screaming, and a moment later, the machine gun went off. He went back to the living room, and Alfredo's wife had been shot about fifteen times with a machine gun. She was still alive, making gurgling noises. Rivi got his pistole and shot her in the back of the head, putting her out of her misery. Miguel, another assassin with Rivi, said he would get paid more money if they could kill the kids, but Rivi fought him and drove them out of the house at gunpoint, leaving the children in the house with their dead parents in the next room. "I said we ain't gonna kill any kids, No, no, no, this is it. It is time to go!" Rivi said.

(*Corben, 2006*)

'Killing my Best Friend" and The Downward Spiral

Griselda didn't trust Carlos Manteco, who was Rivi's best friend. Someone offered Carlos an enormous sum of money to kill Griselda. Rivi found himself in a position where he had to kill Carlos, which he ended up shooting in the head. "To this day, I don't know if Manteco was going to carry out the hit. I doubt it very much because we were too much of friends. For Griselda, all she needed was the doubt," Rivi would say about the murder.

(*Corben, 2006*)

It was around this time that Rivi started living in fear that he might get killed at any time, by someone far more cunning than him. And attempts were made, but he survived. He left the lifestyle and went to Chicago, where he earned a living for himself selling cocaine. Years later, Griselda called him. She said she was at war again and needed him. Some hitmen were after her and her kids. Nobody knows why, but Rivi obliged. He put a crew together to find her enemies and kill them. Rivi was offered a million dollars by her enemies to hand Griselda over, but he was loyal to her and didn't.

Griselda had made too many enemies, and the police were breathing down her neck, she had to leave Miami. So, She did. Things spiraled out of control, and despite his attempt to lay low, police caught Rivi. He was sentenced to life in prison with the possibility of parole after 25 years. He pleaded guilty to the three murders of

Alfredo and Grizel Lorenzo and Johnnie Castro. "*Chucho*" testifying against Griselda Blanco to avoid the death penalty. Rivi is allegedly responsible for over three dozen killings for the Columbina Cartel.

(*Hamacher, 2017*)

CHAPTER 9

TORMENTED SOULS

She franticly ran down the hallway, crashing into the screen door. It wouldn't budge. Time was running out. She desperately pushed against the screen, trying to open it. He was on his way back! If caught, it would be worse, a lot worse.

In the quiet suburbs of Cleveland, Ohio, between 2002 and 2004, a woman and two young girls went missing. Their story would be one of extreme horror and evil. Their disappearances got a lot of media attention because of the extensive resources they used to find them, as well as their age and vulnerability. America's Most Wanted featured the girls in 2004, 2005, and 2006, they also appearing on The Oprah Winfrey Show and The Montel Williams Show. Their communities would help look for them, hold night vigils, and keep a watchful eye for anything that might help reveal where the girls were, but all led nowhere. The women would not be seen again until May 6, 2013, at 2207 Seymour Avenue, about five miles from there last whereabouts. They were all abducted by a man named Ariel Castro. Their story was one of unthinkable horror and torture.

Missing person Report

The first to go missing was Michelle Knight, who disappeared on August 23, 2002. Michelle was scheduled for court on that day for her child's custody case. At the time, she was 21 years old. Michelle enjoyed school as a teen, had a lot of friends, and a talent for sketching. Pregnant at 17, she had to drop out of school. Michelle had dreams of completing her schooling so she could have a better life for her child.

The police did not put much effort into finding Michelle Knight, even when she was reported missing. A social worker assessment concluded Michelle Knight probably ran away after losing the custody case for her son, putting her in distress and unstable state. In hindsight, it is a strange conclusion to come to by the social workers, because Michelle Knight did not take much with her after leaving. The story of her disappearance never got any media attention. The news never featured her in any missing person reports, even though her mother filed a missing person report with her photo and submitted it to the police.

The second girl to disappear was Amanda Berry on April 21, 2003, just a day before her 17th birthday, vanishing after leaving her job at Burger King. The police initially thought Amanda ran away as well. A week later, her father received a call from Amanda's cell phone. In the call, an *unknown man*, who FBI believed to be between the ages of 18 and 30 years old, said, "I have Amanda. She's fine and will be coming home in a couple of days." Amanda's father asked if he could speak to his daughter, but the man abruptly hung up. At first, the FBI thought the call was a hoax, but after discovering the call came from Amanda's phone, they threw out that explanation. FBI agent Robert Hawk stated, "This leads us to believe she was not a runaway. Someone had control of her cell phone."

("Amanda Berry's cell phone…," 2013).

At the time, investigators believed Amanda Berry got into a white sedan with three other men the night she disappeared. This information was made public in hopes of more tips emerging on Amanda's whereabouts. The FBI scoured the area where Amanda was picked up by the sedan, looking for any clues that might lead them to her. At the time, phone tracking wasn't very accurate, so investigators were never able to receive her exact location. Unbeknownst to the authorities, the area they searched would be two blocks away from the house Amanda would later be discovered.

The third missing girl was 14-year-old Gina DeJesus, who disappeared on April 2, 2004, last seen near a payphone around 3 p.m. She was on her way home from school. Police did not issue an Amber Alert for Gina. Angering her father, he responded by saying, "The Amber Alert should work for any missing child.... Whether it's an abduction or a runaway, a child needs to be found. We need to change this law."

("Ariel Castro kidnappings," n.d.).

Ariel Castro

The story of Ariel Castro's kidnappings is infamous because of its starkly disturbing nature. This case also breaks many of the preconceived notions people have about abductions and the people who commit them. Abductions typically happen to naïve people who are unknown to the perpetrators and occur through brute force alone. Ariel Castro was someone whom the victims knew, and the kidnapping occurred in the most innocent of ways, using trust and familiarity as a cloak.

Neighbors described Ariel Castro as cordial. They said he liked to hang out with children in the neighborhood. He was kind, respectful, and private, even described as a decent musician, as he played bass in a local band. No one thought anyone like Ariel would be capable of such monstrosities. No one sensed something as reprehensible as keeping young girls prisoner was happening right in their backyard. Castro was never a suspect and was never under investigation. "Not in my worst nightmare would I have imagined that my brother-in-law would be involved in something like this," said one family member.

(*ABC News, 2013*).

The Mind of a Kidnapper

With how staggering the kidnappings were, people had several questions in mind, but the most prominent was, how did it happen, and what happened while they were there? One journalist describing the way Ariel Castro went about his kidnapping said they were "cliché tactics." While this is true technically, it has the unintended consequence of casting the victims as, for lack of a better word, fools. This idea invokes the "she should have known better" attitude, which plays into one of the biggest myths about kidnappings. This myth implies that the people who get kidnapped should somehow have seen it coming. They usually defend this idea by appealing to myth-based reasoning, like "*don't trust strangers.*"

While never trusting strangers might be a good rule to follow, it is also the sort of thing that allows kidnappers like Ariel Castro to thrive and avoid suspicion. During the girls' disappearance, despite signs that Castro might be a troubled person, he was never suspected. Ariel Castro was a school bus driver, so he knew the children. Castro knew where they went and was very familiar with the neighborhood. He had a history of domestic abuse. He was accused several times of kidnapping his kids.

People like Castro rely on their victim's sense of familiarity and trust to lure them. This notion of trusting people we know plays into the idea, we can predict their behavior, and if we can predict their actions, we often make rational judgments about how much we should trust them. These people also don't have to be people we are close too. They just have to be familiar enough to convince us that we can predict their behavior in a given situation.

Usually, they have been dependable in one area, and we trust that they will not act in ways that are against our interests. A person responsible for driving children to their homes on a school bus fits that category easily. Ariel Castro took advantage of this instinct, consciously or not. Unfortunately, people often overestimate how well they know other people.

Want some puppies?

Michelle Knight was looking for directions to the court-house building she was supposed to go to when Ariel Castro offered her a lift. As soon as Michelle Knight entered the vehicle, Ariel drove in the opposite direction to his house. When Michelle questioned it, Ariel told her he had some puppies for her son at his home. When they arrived, he lured her inside to look at the puppies. That's when things turned quickly. Castro aggressively hogtied Michelle Knight's hands to her feet, carried her to an upstairs bedroom, and left her there.

Need a ride?

Amanda Berry got off work at 7:30 p.m. She called her sister, asking for a ride, but her sister said she would be unable to pick her up. So, Amanda started walking home, and in a nearby parking lot, Amanda saw a familiar man and a girl in a van. She smiled at them and walked past them, a few minutes later, the van pulled over next to her. The man asked if she would like a ride home. Amanda agreed.

In the vehicle, the conversation was cordial and casual. Castro established the similarities they had together. He talked about his son working at Burger King, knowing the employees there, and his daughter, who was classmates with Amanda in middle school. It was then when he asked Amanda if she would like to see his daughter. Amanda agreed, and they drove to his house. When they got inside, Ariel's daughter wasn't there. He told Amanda his daughter must be taking a bath. Castro took Amanda upstairs to show her a woman sitting in a dark room, asleep in front of the television. Amanda Barry, speaking to ABC News, said, "He took me to the next bedroom, and it was just really dark in there, and he didn't turn on the lights, and there was a little, room off of the bigger bedroom, kind of a big closet, he took me in there, and he told me to pull down my pants. From there, I knew this was not going to be good."

(*Diaz, Pearle, & Valiente, 2015*).

Amanda continued to explain how Castro took her to the basement. He taped her ankles and wrists and then put a belt around her ankles. Castro put a helmet on her head and told her if she were quiet, he would take her home. He chained her to a pole, shut off the lights, and left her, with a tv set in the dark. Amanda screamed for help, but nobody came. "I was so scared that I was going to die. I didn't think I was ever going to make it home…" Amanda explained.

(*Diaz, Pearle, & Valiente, 2015*).

Amanda would watch on TV as the story of her disappearance made headlines. She watched her mother and sister on the news pleading and begging for any help and information that could help with finding Amanda. She later stated how seeing her family on TV gave her strength and kept her spirits up. It meant that something was being done to find her.

Let's be Friends

Gina DeJesus was friends with Ariel Castro's daughter Arlene. On the day of her disappearance, Gina was with Arlene. The two were walking home when they stopped at a payphone to ask Arlene's mother if Arlene could sleepover at her house. Her mother refused. Gina was short on money for the bus, so she started walking home from the payphone. A short while later, Castro pulled up at the curb and asked Gina if she had seen his daughter, Arlene. Gina replied that she did, and Arlene was just around the corner. Castro asked Gina if she could help him search for his daughter. She agreed and got into the vehicle with Castro.

He drove her to his house, where he asked Gina for help moving some equipment in the house. Gina felt strange about what was going on. Perhaps being a child in the presence of an adult, Gina felt like she couldn't refuse. Eventually, Castro began touching Gina inappropriately, prompting Gina to ask to leave. He told her she couldn't go the same way she came in and started leading her to the basement. Ariel trapped her and chaining her to a wall. At first, Castro didn't make the chain tight enough, so Gina threw it off and tried to run, but he overpowered her.

The warden

Ariel Castro's kidnappings were crimes of opportunity. This guy wasn't someone who bashed the windows and broke in. He was someone who saw a door open, an empty living room, grabbed the TV, and ran off. A lot of kidnappings happen that way. For the next few years, the girls would live under the tyranny of Ariel Castro's wrath, subjecting them to physical and psychological torture. There was a sadistic streak to him that made him enjoy the more pain he inflicted on his victims. The girls quickly learned to numb themselves from the pain, not to show their emotions. It was little, but something they could take from him in payment for what he took from them.

Castro kept the girls in separate gated rooms. They didn't communicate much with each other when he was around. They often passed notes and pictures through the grates to communicate with each other, only openly talked when he was not around. For much of this time, they were chained to the wall or locked inside. They lived in nervous anticipation of the next rounds of abuse from their tormentor. In their rooms, Castro raped his victims, beat, and tortured them repeatedly. They ate once a day, Castro provided little in the form of clothing, and their showers were limited to once or twice a week. If he weren't particularly happy with one of them, he would starve her, deprive her of baths, or unleash a torrent of violence. Pretty soon, the girls learned to fall in line or face the consequences.

A baby on the way

The conditions in their bedrooms were filthy, with dirty mattresses, a bucket to use as a toilet. These were dehumanizing living conditions.

Castro didn't empty the buckets as often as he should, so it always smelled awful. The young girls forced to endure these conditions for years with only a TV as their only window into the outside world. Castro moved the girls to the TV room as their segment of America's Most Wanted aired wanting them to watch and feel powerless. When Castro's daughter visited, he moved the girls to the basement and told them to be quiet. Fearing the worst, the girls would comply. Talking to ABC News, Gina DeJesus said, "There was always a chance, 'What if he killed everybody?'"

(Diaz, Pearle, & Valiente, 2015).

At the age of 20, Amanda Berry realized she was pregnant. She was terrified, but her child would survive. Amanda gave birth in the house on Christmas, 2006. Castro purchased a small pool so Amanda could give birth in, relying on Michelle to deliver the baby. Michelle Knight became pregnant multiple times by Castro. All ended in miscarriages by the purposeful beatings he gave her. Amanda Berry told ABC News, "Michelle was kind of just talking to me, like, you know, 'Relax. Calm down. You're OK'. And he sat in the rocking chair right there just reading this book about, like, birth and stuff."

(Diaz, Pearle, & Valiente, 2015).

Amanda gave birth to a baby girl, whom she named Jocelyn. Castro treated Jocelyn differently. She was sometimes let out to play in the backyard. He would take her to the park or go to church with her. Castro seemed to show genuine care and love for his daughter. Yet that benevolent side did not transfer and make him treat his prisoners any better. There was no love for his captives.

Turning point

On May 6, 2013, a miracle happened. That day Castro left Berry's bedroom door unlocked, and the front door was open with only the screen door locked shut. He got into his car and left, probably to run some errands.

Jocelyn ran downstairs and returned to her mother. She told her that she didn't find her father downstairs. Berry sensed a moment of opportunity. Heart pounding, shaky, and with a mixture of disbelief and adrenaline. Berry rushed out of her room and went downstairs to the front door. She figured the screen door would be easy to bust open, but it was difficult. She squeezed her arm through and began screaming for help.

A neighbor heard a woman screaming and saw her arm sticking out the door. He approached and helped Amanda break through the lower part of the screen door escaping with her daughter. Amanda ran to Charles

Ramsey's house, the man who helped rescue her, and called 911.

Shortly after this courageous event, Castro was arrested and charged with three counts of rape and four kidnappings. The judge set Castro's bail to $2 million per abduction. On July 26, 2013, Castro pled guilty to "937 criminal counts, including kidnapping, rape, and aggravated murder." He took a plea deal, which helped him avoid the death penalty. The plea deal meant that his victims would not testify in court. The judge sentenced Castro to life without parole and a thousand years in prison.

On September 3, 2013, Ariel Castro committed suicide in his cell at the Correctional Reception Center in Orient, Ohio, using his bedsheets to hang himself. The Ariel Castro kidnappings were shocking and horrific. They led people to wonder if they knew what was going on in their backyards or if they could trust their neighbors and acquaintances. People looked closely at how authorities handled missing person cases. There was a feeling that Michelle Knight would be forgotten if not for the other girls since no one was looking for her anymore.

Castro's crimes were of great injustice. Somehow, even with a sentence as unforgiving as possible, some people were left with the sense that Ariel Castro had taken years away from his victims, that he never really paid for his crimes or fully appreciated the pain he caused. Perhaps the greatest insult to justice was how the man behind the kidnappings revealed just how deluded he had been.

He claimed most of the sex was consensual, that he was a victim of sex and porn addiction, and sometimes the girls asked to have sex with him. He even went so far as to suggest that it was the **FBI**'s fault for not catching him sooner.

CHAPTER 10

THE ABANDONED HOUSE

In an abandoned house near a busy highway, a 22-year-old body of a young woman is found in the most shocking of circumstances, bringing up more questions than answers. The young woman is Gabriela Gomez, a black-haired, brown-eyed, petite freshman at the University of Riverside, last seen alive Thursday night, March 8, 2007, a year and a half before anyone would find her body.

Orientation

Gabriela was reported missing on March 10, 2007, by her parents. Fellow students described Gabriela Gomez as bright and bubbly. She was part of the chess team. She volunteered at the Riverside Animal Shelter and spent her spare time socializing with friends. "The story of Gabriela Gomez is essentially a two-part story," Said Cheryl Cohen Senior Reporter at the Riverside Press-Enterprise, speaking to True Crime Weekly. She had been responsible for covering the story for the Press-Enterprise. "It's not a classic girl-gone-missing story. The first part is very much that story, then you get to the second part, and you realize this is something a lot like a Karin Slaughter book."

When an academic year at university starts, first-year students go through orientation. During this period, the girls usually have a different section of orientation from the boys. The university informs students about staying safe on and off-campus. Universities know a lot can go wrong on campus, and when you are a young woman, you are even more vulnerable. They talk about making sure the girls never walk home alone at night, to stay in groups at parties, to get into cars with people they trust, and to watch their drinks in unfamiliar places or when very far from home—the golden rules of staying safe as a female student.

The very first weekend after orientation, the seniors come back, and the entire campus erupts. Students fill the bars, and streets are run over by club hoppers, this is what all those years of hard work in high school had been leading. The seniors are integral to this change because they know the city better, they have made connections with locals, and if they host a party or arrange a night of heavy drinking, it quickly becomes a large get-together. That was the same story with Riverside, both the city and the university. "It almost seems as if they forgot the lessons from orientation,"

Cheryl said. But when you look closely, you see the students do follow them pretty well. Gabriela was one of those girls who stuck to those guidelines. She got along quickly with people but didn't trust easily. Always kept in groups, never walked alone at night, and never got too drunk, which makes the night of her disappearance almost too strange.

Missing

On Thursday night, March 8, 2007, Gabriela Gomez leaves her dorm around 8 pm and heads to a popular local bar, Worthingtons Sports Bar, close to her dorm. Witnesses say she stayed there for a while, had a few drinks, and left. Gabriela had been alone. She was heading to a party a few blocks from the bar at her friend Christie's apartment."You can imagine she felt safe there. The place was relatively close, and there was always an option that if she got drunk, she could stay there, or her friends would take her home. So even by campus recommended safety guidelines, there was no reason to be overly cautious," Said Cheryl.

It is a night of heavy drinking and rapturous partying. Around midnight Gabriela leaves the party. Witnesses say they saw her walking in the opposite direction, away from Christie's apartment and the safety of the campus. It wasn't strange to see students leaving parties at that time of night and heading south, where the better clubs are. Often parties at apartments serve as pre-drinking gatherings. What is unusual in this case is that it was a Thursday. Most clubs are closed, and club-hopping doesn't work all that well. Locals usually frequent the open bars, and the students who go here during these nights are frequently seniors or postgrad students who have also assimilated into the Riverside community's culture.

Witnesses say they saw Gabriela around 12:30 pm, stumbling down University avenue away from Christie's apartment when she got into a black sedan. On March 11, 2007, when it became apparent, she was missing, the Riverside Police Department launched a search, with students and locals as volunteers. The search took them to rivers, lakes, abandoned complexes, and shadier parts of the city but, in the end, turns up nothing.

Suspects

The first suspect was Elias Mendoza, a male friend, who seemed to like Gomez, almost a little awkwardly. Friends say Elias would find excuses and ways of bumping into Gabriela whenever he was free. "It was borderline stalking at first. Then as the friendship grew, it became a quirk," one friend said.

It was easy to do. At the University of Riverside, students can use the student portal to find each other if they know each other's student numbers. For Elias, this would have been easy as he shared one class with Gabriela. The information provided on the portal would be the student's dorm, classroom, and contact information. Friend's suspect he used the portal to get her class schedule, making sure he was nearby when she was free. Elias claimed that the night of her disappearance, he saw Gabriela stumbling down University avenue, picked her up, and took her to her dorm room where he left her sleep off the alcohol.

The second suspect was Mark Guzman, another student at the party the night of Gabriela's disappearance. He claims to have just seen her walk out of the party around midnight. But police found his school ID in Gabriela's dorm room. Establishing the relationship between Mark Guzman, an athletic, tall young man with a sharp jaw and crewcut, became evident. "Mark was well known as a bit of a trouble-maker, the normal kind – not anything criminal; young, confident, a partier, you sense with him things regularly got extreme," Said Cheryl.

When asked about his relationship with Gabriela, he said they weren't friends, he didn't know her very well and didn't interact with her outside of the party. When asked about the Id card, he said he did not know how it got there. Police looked carefully but could not establish any link between him and her disappearance. The cops talked to everyone, her chess club, the animal shelter where she volunteered, and her friends, but nothing came up.

In the meantime, students plastered missing person's posters of a smiling Gabriela throughout campus and the city. And nothing. Police set up a tip line, and thousands of tips came pouring in. And still nothing. Her parents, Angie and Miguel Gomez appeared on TV, anguished and cheeks glistening with tears, appealing to anyone who knew anything. No one came forward. Months pass, with each an ever-increasing feeling of hopelessness and dread. The longer people go missing, the worse and more graphic people's thoughts become. Their imaginations have a lot of time to explore even the darkest of possibilities. Most of the time, it is not as horrific as imagined, although it may be something horrible. In this case, unfortunately, those imaginations couldn't have been more real.

Crime Scene

It wasn't until a year and a half later, in the autumn of 2008, when they found Gabriela Gomez's body 15 miles away from where she disappeared. A couple looking to buy property smelled something putrid coming from an abandoned house. They felt like something was wrong, so they called the police. Nothing could have prepared officers for what they saw. Inside were the remains of Gabriela Gomez, her mummified corpse lying in the middle of a pentagram-like symbol drawn in blood.

They also found animal blood and chicken bones near her body, which led them to suspect something ritualistic had taken place. Cause of death? Blunt force trauma to the head, with fractures to the ribs and right leg. The owner of the abandoned house said he left a few months before the couple found the body when asked. He became an immediate suspect, but nothing connected him to Gabriela Gomez. Detective Taylor, who was in charge of the investigation, was concerned, "Who could have done something so disturbing. "It became evident to the police that whoever took Gabriela had kept her alive for months. The person was possibly close by, watching everything.

This kind of thing takes quite a bit of determination. The person who did this acted alone or as part of a small group, considering the type of space and control required to hide someone for months. A visibly exhausted Detective Taylor said in a news conference. "This leads us to believe that whoever has done this is someone in the community. Someone who is a local possibly and between the ages of 30 to 50."

Desperate for clues, they turned to Phillip Maher, a Religious Studies professor who is an expert in cults and spiritualism. The hope was that the professor's expertise would narrow down their search to specific groups or areas, and help them make better sense of the crime scene.

The dilemma was, there was no known cult movement in the area. The crime scene we usually see in this kind of practice wasn't apparent. "I've never seen anything like it," said Professor Maher, speaking recently at a TV interview.

A Sacrifice

That was the first problem Maher noticed. If this was something ritualistic, then what has happened here is sacrificial. The problem with that is you don't get many sacrificial rituals where the sacrificial animal isn't beat to death. Blood has to be spilled, which makes Gabriela's case strange if we say she is a sacrifice. They spilled the chicken's blood, now that tells us something. But what? The blood which makes the pentagram doesn't come from Gabriela or the chicken. It is from an animal, not at the crime scene. That was the second problem. None of the imagery, the symbols, the slaughtered chicken, or Gabriela's body points to anything known about these sorts of practices.

It is a hodgepodge of various influences that don't meld well together. Either this is a smokescreen or someone who felt some remorse and thought doing this would absolve them somehow. But whoever this person is, they don't belong to a defined group. Someone who batters someone to death acts out of an impulse, not careful planning, and rituals are all about the plan, doing things the proper way. This crime scene wasn't any of that; the method of death was aggressive.

A crime scene is supposed to illuminate some mystery to the officers. This one did that, but some remained. It helped the officers form a different suspect in their minds and tell a plausible enough story of what happened to Gabriela. At least questions that were pertinent to solving the case and catching the person responsible. There were other, more personal questions about the event. For instance, what was Gabriela's day-to-day experience of her capture? What was the relationship between her and her capturer? And did she suffer until her death? Answering these questions could help the police, if only they could find the place where Gabriela was kept, or even better, the person who had done it.

Dead ends

The first thing they did was look at a list of previous offenders who lived nearby. These were usually people convicted of assault and other violent offenses, including homicide. They turned up nothing, either in prison when she disappeared, their alibi checked out, or their searches produced nothing that cleared up the case any further. The police searched the area, asked neighbors if they'd seen or heard anything. Opened a tip line for any information about anyone who fit the profile.

A new batch of tips poured in, and again the police got nothing. It was now starting to get a little hopeless at this point. Officers on the case, felt a sense of defeat creeping in. Nothing much had changed. Usually, when a body turns up, the body talks, the scene talks, and cases get solved quickly. There was a sense that the same thing would be happening here. So they kept returning to the scene. The police went back to the crime scene for more clues. There, staring back at them, was a clue they overlooked. The person who did this might have access to live animals. Perhaps they worked on or owned a farm. That would explain how someone like Gabriela could disappear for so long without anyone noticing. It would be easier to hide on a big farm, not too many eyes. There was such a place on the outskirts of the city, Herman's Farms.

Herman's Farms produced chickens and goats. While it is relatively simple to get live chickens to slaughter, the pentagram would require a lot more blood than a chicken could provide. The farm owners cooperated and didn't seem to be anything on their farm or home that pointed to them. The police moved on to the employees, and they found what looked like their man, 32-year-old Killian Parker.

Killian fits the profile in many ways. He had a particular interest in spiritualism and cults. Killian lived alone in a house less than 2 miles from where police found Gabriela. He showed an interest in occult symbols and art. The police went to his house in Sunny View Street. When asked where he was the night Gabriela disappeared,

Killian said he didn't remember, that Killian was probably at home and always at home when not at work or running errands. "Neighbors described him as reclusive. He never said hi to anyone, always wearing black when not working, hardly got any visitors, never participated in any of the neighborhood activities, seemed like he was lonely." Said, Cheryl. He denied the police entry, stating his rights. The police would come back with a search warrant in hand two days later. The minute they entered, occult imagery was everywhere.

There were posters of goat head pentagrams on the walls, a collection of black metal music with disturbing cover art, Wiccan sacrificial knives, and other dark material. The police searched for any sign that someone might have been kept prisoner for months, but they found no signs except BDSM equipment. They found a head harness with a ball gag, a sleep sack, armbinder, bondage cuffs, and much more. They also found hair. The BDSM stuff is bizarre because reportedly, Killian lived alone and hardly had any visitors. But if he were to kidnap someone, all this stuff would come in handy.

There's more. Killian was receiving treatment from the Riverside Mental Health Clinic for an undisclosed personality disorder. Killian had shown anger problems in the past, one time getting arrested for assault, but the court dismissed the charges. He was also a member of an anger management group. Killian, unable to establish a concrete timeline and an alibi, was arrested on suspicion of kidnapping and murder. "At this point, it looks like the police have their guy," Said Cheryl.

On his computer, the police found a stream of extreme porn images and videos, some of them bordering on abuse. The police scoured through his finances and bills, computer documents, and receipts, anything that might divulge more information. Killian kept a lot of receipts. They thought if they went through his expenses over two years, they would find a change. If you hold someone hostage, you will spend; differently, it would show in your purchases one way or the other. It was here that the police ran into a problem; there was nothing out of the ordinary. The hair they found in the house didn't belong to Gabriela either. If Killian was guilty of anything is that he was strange. The police went in there already convinced it was their guy. They overlooked other pieces of evidence that clearly showed that Killian couldn't be the guy. Among other things, he was actively working on his mental health and making progress.

In the bills and receipt for Killian, there is one for a hospital stay at Riverside Hospital between March 8 and March 10, 2007. He had an appendectomy. A procedure like that would have taken him one to three weeks to recover from and get back to work fully. This documentation meant Killian couldn't be the person who had kidnapped Gabriela, and by extension, not the person who killed her either. The police are back where they started, with a lot more questions than answers.

In the end, there wasn't enough evidence to convict or connect anyone to the crime. Gabriela Gomez's mysterious kidnapping, murder, and the strange crime scene will puzzle authorities to this day. What the story of

Gabriela illustrates is the limitations of safety guidelines for young women in colleges. There have to be real protections in place, more surveillance, and security. Perhaps this wouldn't have happened. The case currently remains open.

CONCLUSION

True crime stories pique our interest because of their mystery. Even solved cases still hold details or questions around the motive, that continue to have us wondering decades after the person committed the crime. True crime is about our humanity. It is the answer to the question: How do people become evil? We focus so intently on this content, perhaps because we hope that it will help us to avoid becoming victims or even maybe perpetrators.

The cases presented in this book represent a wide range of victims and scenarios. Many of them illustrate serious inequities in society, such as the case of the murdered Bowraville children. Sadly, such invisible victims are not unique to Australia; the phenomenon occurs all over the world, and both children and adults are affected. Such inequities, when valuable evidence is lost, create mystery. The real crime is that such evidence is not just good for proving guilt but also innocence. Besides the actual victims of crimes, how many more victims sit in jail for the rest of their lives, having been found guilty of crimes they did not commit simply because of poorly carried out investigations.

The unique case of Gareth Williams shields the public from tales of spy assassinations and the like. Simply based on the way this murder played out, it moved into the public domain resulting in journalists tying threads of other cases together. Perhaps several intelligence agencies would have preferred to be left alone. We need to maintain focus on cases like Gareth's, though, because despite what he did for a living, he deserves justice as much as anyone else. If we ignore cases like his, we profile the value of the victim because he was a spy, in the same way as profiling the Bowraville children for being Aboriginal, and coming from a poor community. Justice does not have a skin color, ethnicity, or occupation. Justice should be for all.

The power of DNA, specifically familial DNA, is a massive buzzword in the true crime community right now. One of the most infamous serial killer cases of all time, The Golden State Killer, was solved thanks to a familial DNA match. If it weren't for that technology, the victims of Joseph James DeAngelo would likely have never gotten justice, and his specter would have haunted the world long after he passed away peacefully surrounded by family. Thanks to familial DNA, he will not get that privilege, because he has not earned it. Instead, he will serve the rest of his days behind bars, where he belongs. Familial DNA also helped the family of Milica van Doorn to find closure. In that case, justice is perhaps questionable as Milica's murderer will walk the streets again. What was gained from that case, though, was a semblance of peace. They closed the book on a case that horrified them for decades. The police officers who so tirelessly worked her case can say they did their jobs and caught the monster who took a young girl's life. Many states within America and countries across the world are now looking at their legislation as it relates to familial DNA, and we could look forward to seeing many more cold cases solved in the future thanks to this science.

Evil is an interesting concept, but it certainly isn't a scientifically definable one. Most often, psychiatry and psychology can help to provide us with the answers as to why an offender does what they do. In some cases, though, a sequence of events — call it fate if you will — comes together in just the right way to create a coupling that is so complicated even forensic science fails to understand its nature truly. Fred and Rosemary West were one such coupling, and the horrifying coincidence that caused them to meet would send ripples through the lives of all who knew them. Individually, they were disturbed enough, but together, they played off each other's strengths and weaknesses in such a way they became an almost unstoppable source of pain for the world. Such pairings, while rare, do occur throughout the years.

Another UK example was Ian Brady and Myra Hindley, who sexually assaulted and murdered children between 1963 and 1965. A famous Australian serial killer couple committed the crimes known as the Moorhouse murders in 1986. David and Catherine Birnie killed four women and attempted to murder a fifth in the space of five weeks. Karla Homolka and Paul Bernado were Canada's answer to Fred and Rosemary, and they killed three women, including Karla's sister. It is rare for serial killers to work in pairs, and when they do, it is often with an intimate partner. Fred and Rose West were found guilty, and their known victims received justice, but there are still so many questions around this couple. It is difficult for us to say whether this case will ever indeed be closed in the mind of the public, at least.

Families of missing people who have later been found murdered, often admit that it is far more difficult not to know where your loved one is than to know that they are deceased. Under the pressure of having a missing loved one, marriages dissolve, it destroys families, and even becomes challenging to maintain friendships. Not knowing is far worse than knowing. For the family of Tammy Kingery, they had to deal with the pain of not knowing for six years, turning her husband into a single father. Her children are having to live with the pain of not knowing what happened to their mother. Todd Kohlhepp sits in prison with his secrets and refuses to provide more information about the additional victims he claims to have murdered. Whether he holds the key to Tammy's disappearance or not is unknown, but he does hold the key that will unlock answers for other families. Despite this, he refuses to provide further information and holds on to his tiny little piece of control and denies family peace. Missing person cases are perhaps some of the greatest mysteries in true crime. It is terrifying to think that one can be living their life one minute and the next, simply disappear off the face of the earth. No one ever really disappears, though, and in every case, there is at least one person who knows something. The key is to find that person and extract their truth.

While tales of true crime are fascinating to us for many reasons, the predominant reason for their retelling should always be to share the victim's story. When someone falls foul of a person with evil intentions, they lose not just their life but often their voice. Even if they have loved ones and a justice system who's there to stand up for them, they become just a name on a piece of paper far too often. Proof of this is that we can name many killers, and, more often than not, we cannot name even one of their victims. Perhaps, with true crime podcasts, books, and YouTube channels providing more information about the victims, this can begin to shift. As consumers of this material, we can also make a difference by supporting creators that focus on the victims and do not glorify the offender while still providing balanced and informative coverage. We can also help to shift the narrative by refusing to be part of a society that condones the *invisible victim* phenomenon and encouraging mainstream media to cover cases that are not only guaranteed to increase clicks but also to give the victims a voice.

The world that we live in is now more open to the awareness of social issues than ever before. We can spread awareness of cases to all corners of the globe without even leaving our armchair. The growth of the true-crime community has led to an increase in leads, especially in cold cases, and higher identification rates of Jane and John Does. As people become more knowledgeable about familial DNA, we hope a higher number of people will start to submit their DNA to databases to help solve crimes. Crowdsourcing of volunteers to compile databases has also become more popular now that people with interest in true crime have a helpful channel in which to direct their efforts. The true-crime community can make a significant difference in aiding in the resolution of cases, as long as they are responsible. You will have noted that, in this book, where facts based on witness accounts or rumor and a perpetrator not found guilty, we use words such as "allegedly" and "claimed." This terminology is to protect people from false allegations. It is not uncommon, especially in complex cold cases.

For a person to be accused wrongly of being guilty, and where there is no proof of guilt, there can still be a desire found by the court of public opinion. Many people live large parts of their lives under a cloud of suspicion due to unfair reporting and sensationalism. Park Ringery experienced that when his wife, Tammy, disappeared. Although he had an airtight alibi and there was never any proof he was involved in his wife's disappearance, he has had his every action and statement scrutinized and blown out of proportion by the mainstream media and the public. He is one of many people across the world who experience this phenomenon, and it is vital that we, as a true-crime community, do not perpetuate this sort of behavior and stigma. In any interactions you have online, whether about the cases we discussed or any other, it is important to share only facts and when sharing opinions to do so very carefully and be clear that it is your view on the matter. Doing this ensures less made up interference in a case and that there is a higher likelihood that victims will get justice.

The consumption of true crime content can be an exciting hobby to partake in, and it can also play a very positive role in the resolution of these cases when appropriately undertaken. It is always important to remember, though, that these victims have families and people who love them. Things that you say online could very well be read or seen by someone who loved the victim, and it is crucial to be mindful of this. The perpetrator has a family too, and while it is entirely reasonable for us to express our rage at the offender, their actions do not extend to their parents, siblings, or children and, where possible, those people should be kept out of the narrative as much as possible.

We have covered some tragic stories in *Hannah J Tidy's True Crime Stories*, but we would prefer you not to leave with a sense of tragedy. Every time we read the story of a victim, their memory is kept alive. Their families do not want the world to forget their loved ones. We also leave a story having learned about how people become victims and perpetrators. If we use this knowledge to work within our communities, help children who are in difficult situations, and people are in abusive or dangerous relationships, we can use these stories to make the world a better place — one true crime story at a time.

REFERENCES

(n.d.). https://soundcloud.com/the-australian-1/bowraville-episode-1-the-murders

Anonym. (n.d.). How a brother led to suspicious murder Milica van Doorn | tellerreport.com. Www.Tellerreport. Com. Retrieved March 23, 2020, from https://www.tellerreport.com/news/--how-a-brother-led-to-suspicious-murder-milica-van-doorn-.ryBnIVy0Q.html

Blake, T. W., Jason Leopold, Alex Campbell, Richard Holmes, Jane Bradley, Heidi. (n.d.). The Death Of The Spy In The Bag Is One of 14 Suspected Hits Linked To Russia. BuzzFeed. Retrieved March 23, 2020, from https://www.buzzfeed.com/tomwarren/secrets-of-the-spy-in-the-bag?utm_term=.vc0qkoMmX#.lobLpoKwm

Bray, A. (2019, January 31). The gruesome details of Fred and Rose West murders revealed. Devonlive. https://www.devonlive.com/news/celebs-tv/gruesome-details-fred-rose-west-2491388

Buckland, L. (2018, September 17). Fred and Rose West's daughter makes chilling prediction about their victims. Mirror. https://www.mirror.co.uk/tv/tv-news/fred-wests-daughter-believes-could-13258208

Finn, H. (2019, July 29). ID Channel Series Investigates Whether Serial Killer Todd Kohlhepp Had More Victims

Than We Know. Good Housekeeping. https://www.
goodhousekeeping.com/life/entertainment/a28435680/
todd-kohlhepp-serial-killer-devil-unchained/

Fred West. (2014, April 2). Biography. https://www.
biography.com/crime-figure/fred-west

Hamer, D. (n.d.). How the law failed three children and their
families in the Bowraville murder case. The Conversation.
Retrieved March 22, 2020, from https://theconversation.
com/how-the-law-failed-three-children-and-their
-families-in-the-bowraville-murder-case-103330

Kindon, F. (2019, February 21). Incest, abuse and
murder - the true story of Fred and Rose West's children.
Mirror. https://www.mirror.co.uk/tv/tv-news/fred-rose
-wests-children-who-13927960

Lo, T. (2019, October 19). Serial killers Rose West
and Myra Hindley were "lovers in prison for months."
Mirror. https://www.mirror.co.uk/news/uk-news/
serial-killers-rose-west-myra-20651910

Murphy, N. (2018, September 1). Fred and Rose
West's daughter describes life growing up in "House
of Horrors." Mirror. https://www.mirror.co.uk/news/
uk-news/fred-rose-wests-daughter-describes-13174021

News, N. B. C. (n.d.). UPDATE: Suspect in Kala Brown
Abduction Case Confesses to 4 Murders: Sheriff. Www.
Wsaz.Com. Retrieved March 27, 2020, from https://
www.wsaz.com/content/news/Body-Found-on-Property

-Where-Woman-Held-Chained-IDd-as-Missing-Boyfriend-400142051.html

Scheikowski, M. (2018, September 13). No retrial over Bowraville murders | timeline of events. Newcastle Herald. https://www.newcastleherald.com.au/story/5645017/no-retrial-over-bowraville-murders-timeline-of-events/

Spy in the bag: The mysterious death of Gareth Williams | Journal Online. (2018, September 22). Journal.Com. Ph. https://journal.com.ph/editorial/mysteries/spy-bag-mysterious-death-gareth-williams

Todd Kohlhepp. (2019, July 8). The Murder Squad. http://themurdersquad.com/episodes/todd-kohlhepp/

Twenty years in prison for 1992 Zaandam murder. (2018, December 11). NL Times. https://nltimes.nl/2018/12/11/twenty-years-prison-1992-zaandam-murder

Wahlquist, C. (2016, May 23). Australia's Serial: Dan Box on the making of true crime podcast Bowraville. The Guardian. https://www.theguardian.com/media/2016/may/23/australias-serial-dan-box-on-the-making-of-true-podcast-bowraville

WHERE IS TAMMY KINGERY? | MIDWEEK MYSTERY. (2018). [YouTube Video]. In YouTube. https://www.youtube.com/watch?v=53dowM6ojy

Kessler, M. (2011, September 1). What Happened To Mitrice Richardson? Los Angeles Magazine. Los

Angeles Magazine. https://www.lamag.com/longform/what-happened-to-mitrice-richardson/

Trace Evidence - 066 - The Mysterious Death of Mitrice Richardson. (2019). [YouTube Video]. On YouTube. https://www.youtube.com/watch?v=UotZzU6dtzo

ABC News. (2013, May 7). *Cleveland abduction suspect's family shocked by arrest* [Video]. ABC News. https://abcnews.go.com/WNT/video/cleveland-abduction-suspects-family-shocked-arrest-19128934

Amanda Berry's cell phone used a week after she went missing (republished story). (2013, May 1). Retrieved from Cleveland.com: https://www.cleveland.com/metro/2013/05/amanda_berrys_cell_phone_used.html

Ariel Castro kidnappings. (n.d.). Retrieved from Wikipedia: https://en.wikipedia.org/wiki/Ariel_Castro_kidnappings#cite_note-usat072613-8

Diaz, J., Pearle, L., & Valiente, A. (2015, April 27). What Life in Captivity Was Like for Cleveland Kidnapping Survivors Amanda Berry and Gina DeJesus. Retrieved from ABC News: https://abcnews.go.com/US/life-captivity-cleveland-kidnapping-survivors-amanda-berry-gina/story?id=30532737

Retrieved from ABC News: https://abcnews.go.com/WNT/video/cleveland-abduction-suspects-family-shocked-arrest-19128934

Corben, B. (Director). (2006). Cocaine Cowboys [Motion Picture].

Hamacher, B. (2017, April 13). South Florida's Most Notorious 'Cocaine Cowboys'. Retrieved from NBC6: https://www.nbcmiami.com/news/local/south-floridas-most-notorious-cocaine-cowboys/11254/

60 Minutes Australia. *Inside the depraved world of David and Louise Turpin.* (2019). Retrieved from https://www.youtube.com/watch?v=_lcPhyMb5cc&t=203s

Inside Edition. *Turpin' House of Horrors' 911 Call: 'We Live in Filth.'* (2019). Retrieved from https://www.youtube.com/watch?v=lFg955I743E

Killelea, E. (2018, June 25). Nightmare in California: What We Know About Allegedly Tortured Siblings. Retrieved April 15, 2020, from https://www.rollingstone.com/culture/culture-news/nightmare-in-perris-california-what-we-know-about-allegedly-tortured-siblings-201993/